OLD KETTERING
- A VIEW FROM
THE 1930s

Book 3

Kettering's Victorian drinking fountain, over 100 years old, illustrates social history. Shoe manufacturer John Bryan developed the Rockingham Road Park area, and gave the fountain for the park. Many people remember as children pressing the button to fill a chained cup. Then it was vandalised and removed as unsafe in 1972. Thirteen years later, its beauty and interest realised, it was re-erected in Dalkeith Place. But it's dry — water is still out of fashion in these more-affluent days.

(Fred Moore)

OLD KETTERING - A VIEW FROM THE 1930s

Book 3

TONY IRESON

For Dr. John Notley with sincere thanks for his help, and every good wish, from

Tony Ireson

22. XI. 92

Published by the author and printed by
Woolnough Bookbinding Ltd
Irthlingborough, Northamptonshire

1992

ISBN 0 9509800 3 X

By the same author:

NORTHAMPTONSHIRE
  Robert Hale County Books

OLD KETTERING AND ITS DEFENDERS

OLD KETTERING – A VIEW FROM THE 1930s
  Book 1

OLD KETTERING – A VIEW FROM THE 1930s
  Book 2

Typeset in 10/12pt Melliza by Gilcott Graphics, Rushden, Northamptonshire

CONTENTS

ILLUSTRATIONS

INTRODUCTION

As with previous Old Kettering books, this one aims to record events of 50 and more years ago before they are forgotten, and to evoke memories from readers. It recalls childhood, home life and schooldays, describes theatres and cinemas for which we once queued, remembers the wonderful pre-NHS voluntary work of the hospital, nursing and ambulance services, relates some family histories, and includes a wide selection of personal recollections.

To set the scene briefly, life in the 1920s and 1930s was vastly different though lived in streets that have changed little. Mass motoring had not arrived, the streets were clear of cars, and they served as playgrounds. Children played across-the-road cricket with chalked wickets and up-and-down football with piled coats for goalposts, but always with an old tennis ball out of consideration for passers-by. A host of other games, and exploits with scooters, roller skates, soap box chariots, catapults and bows and arrows were constant sources of amusement and exercise. I look back with gratitude on the tolerance of the older generation who endured flying missiles, broken glass and squashed garden plants with a forbearance that has surely earned them places in heaven.

Our street, The Grove, was rough and unmade, enriched with manure from delivery horses, and either blowing dust or dotted with puddles. Children were always falling over and going home with hands and bare knees lacerated, but mother's bathing with Condy's fluid, plus a safety-pinned bandage, quickly returned the battered warrior to the fray.

The atmosphere in winter was at times appalling as chimneys poured out smoke. The electricity works had an enormous chimney where Sainsbury's stands, and there were dozens more at places like the gas works, the brickyard in London Road, the Furnaces, Wilmot's laundry in Church Walk and many factories. Smoke blew across the town from the railway engine sheds, and hundreds of domestic chimneys added their sooty quota. The result was pea-souper fogs in which you could only see a few yards ahead by day, and at night steered your way through the suffocating murk by blobs of light from street lamps.

Life seemed rich in relationships. Everybody knew everybody because we walked or cycled about the town exchanging greetings instead of riding sealed in cars. Schoolboys, on bikes or afoot, raised their caps to their masters and to ladies. Shabbiness had not become a cult. Everybody aimed to be well-groomed, and women with hats, gloves and parasols always looked like ladies, never wearing anything unbecoming.

There was a stimulating community life in the evenings, when meetings were important gatherings, held to promote causes, to hear serious lectures, or to debate vital issues. There was informed interest in local government with Council meetings a major attraction, at times of tension attended by a policeman to keep the listening ratepayers in order. Local government was local. Councillors and officials walked the town, talked to people and inspected sources of complaint. Policemen patrolled their beats, making regular points, and were known to people in their patch, while the inspector and superintendent were often about on foot, taking a paternal interest in good behaviour. The magistrates court, scene of many legal dramas, was a well-attended spectacle.

Other meeting places were at the Poppies' games, to which supporters walked up Rockingham Road in a solid phalanx, at town centre pubs and clubs midday and evenings, and at the churches, as most people seemed to be attached to some place of worship, even if it was only "the one they didn't go to." Kettering had about 30 churches, chapels and meeting houses, earning it the nickname of "the Holy City." Bands paraded the town, notably the Salvation Army which held services with stentorian preachers at such natural assembly points as the top of Gas Street and the top of Northall. They were an inspiring sight on the march. Now they go round in cars, and I am told can't get the big drum in, so don't take it.

Almost everyone who lived in the town worked in the town.

Their jobs brought people into contact every day, and the streets of terraced houses were the homes of established families who befriended one another. At many points the houses of the rich were only yards from those of the not-so-rich, but I never noticed any jealousy or ill-feeling. In a self-made working class town everybody had a chance. Some were high flyers and some weren't — it was just the way the cookie crumbled.

A few women figured in public life, but most were too busy at home. Families needed three cooked meals a day, cleaning had to be done without modern aids, the weekly wash was a gruelling ritual, and besides running the home, acting as nurse to an extended family, and sometimes helping out at a part-time job, women fulfilled their destiny as wives and mothers, producing the next generation and giving the children as good a start as they could. From hard experience they developed wisdom and judgement to which husbands with sense deferred, so that mother was more often than not the power in the household.

At school there was no time-wasting. Children knew they were there to learn and everyone respected masters and mistresses who did not spare themselves in their work for the pupils, in and out of school hours. Basic education was sound — tables, grammar, correct speech and above all manners. Parents were alive to the wiles of their offspring, and supported the teachers in their determination that every child leaving school should be literate, numerate, and know right from wrong.

Winters were severe, and it was a cold world in the four months around Christmas. We had to wear warm underclothing and day outfits, with thick overcoats almost to the ankles, gloves, scarves and hats, and there were even pocket handwarmers. Snow and ice, almost forgotten today, could persist for weeks. There was usually only one fire at home with everybody sitting round it, and upstairs rooms in most houses were like ice, with going to bed a polar expedition, especially when meeting the shock of chilly sheets. There were water jugs and basins for washing but the water might be frozen when you woke. Chamber pots were under the beds for emergencies, as most lavatories were out in the backyards, and it was not unusual to sit there contemplating with the snow blowing in under the door. Bathing meant using a tin bath before the kitchen fire, unless you made the trip to the Council's slipper baths off Bath Road.

Because the £ was worth so much in those days we had a magnificent currency, and there was real affection for the notes and coins. A solemnly unfolded outsize £5 note, black on white bank paper, was a fortune indeed, and there were green £1 and red-brown 10s notes. Until George VI the large and elegant half-crown, eight to the £1, and the florin, shilling, sixpence and threepenny bit were silver alloy, and with the bronze penny, halfpenny and farthing provided for division of the £ by multiples of 2, 3, and 5 down to the farthing, which was roughly a thousandth of £1. A reminder of the silver coinage is the threepenny bit, still making an appearance in Christmas puddings. Instead of pocket calculators we had amazing publications called Ready Reckoners in which all likely calculations were done for you, and the answers given in columns of type.

In mentioning money, I do not give the decimal equivalents, as they would be entirely misleading. For example, the old age pension was 10s a week, half of £1, but that was not equal to 50 pence today. Its real value was more like £50, which gives some idea of what inflation has done. The *Evening Telegraph* was 1d in the 1930s, and you could buy the paper for 40 weeks for £1. Now £1 buys it for four days. At the other end of the scale, you can look at present-day advertisements for houses, knock off the last two noughts from the price, and still arrive at rather more than the value in 1930s £1 notes.

Getting about was easier, with no real need to own a car, even if you could afford one. Railways ran everywhere and gave a dependable service for passengers, parcels and goods to hundreds of stations along main and rural routes at reasonable rates. Northamptonshire, crossed by five main lines interlinked by country branches, had nearly 80 stations in 1923, and there were still nearly 50 in 1960, but after the Beeching cuts only six survived. Railway travel was supplemented by excellent bus services, radiating at Kettering from standings at the Library, and cycling was pleasant and safe.

I have many people to thank for generous help. Fred Moore, Malcolm Robinson and the Public Library reference room have been infallible sources, and among those who have contributed reminiscences, often written at length, are John Andrew, Jim

Dodge, David Bradshaw, Philip Hague, Pete Hanger, Don Sinclair, Eva Starmer, Margaret Baish, Gertrude Williams, Marjorie Wright, Douglas Ashby, Ted Grove, Mary Cooper and Reg Tailby. I have made use of Colin Ball's theatre history. Dr Drake-Lee's memories lent by Dr John Smith have been a first-hand source, and the General Hospital, District Nurses and St John have all been helpful. Christopher Gotch, David Squire, Doris Butlin and Ted Wright, representatives of the families described, have provided records, and other friends helped in many ways, especially by lending photographs or checking parts of the text.

From the past I turn to the future. The A1-M1 link, the only east-west motorway-standard road between the M25 and M62, has placed Kettering firmly at the crossroads of the country and opened the way to development. A new Kettering is springing up along it. The Council is committed to attracting industry and commerce, encouraging business expansion, and helping firms to move from the old town. Locations for development are Telford Way, Pytchley Lodge Industrial Estate, Kettering Venture Park, Kettering Business Park, Weekley Woods Business Park, Glendon Employment Park, Burton Latimer Business and Industrial Park, and Desborough and Rothwell Industrial Parks.

The shape of things to come is shown by the establishment of the RCI Europe headquarters, the 88-bedroom Kettering Park Hotel, and the £13m Leisure Village. The Village, funded by Kettering Council and Redelco together, will rival any sports centre in the country. It will have a floodlit artificial pitch for hockey and football, a full-size grass pitch and an eight-lane running track, and tennis courts with an inflatable cover for year-round use. Indoors will be a pool with the latest refinements, an ice rink, a dance and aerobics studio, a health and fitness suite, meeting rooms, four squash courts, a county standard gym, a hall for netball, badminton and volleyball, facilities for bowling and snooker, an arena for exhibitions and a golf simulator enabling you to play a computer-video round whatever the weather.

RCI, the world's largest and oldest holiday exchange network which arranges holiday travel for about six million people annually, has built its Europe headquarters on an eight-acre site. A staff of 500 serves 210,000 British and European members, handles some 16,000 phone calls a day organising time-share holiday exchanges all over the world, and has a transatlantic link to the main headquarters at Indianapolis. Rather than expand in London the firm took advice as to the best provincial site and came to Kettering. They are delighted with the calibre of the staff.

The four-star Kettering Park Hotel by Shire Inns has conference and banqueting facilities, restaurant, bars, swimming and spa pools, a sauna, solarium, steam room, squash courts and snooker and exercise areas. Many other buildings are taking shape.

When the last A1-M1 stretch across Naseby battlefield is completed and the link joins the Midlands with the East Coast ports, thousands of vehicles will flow daily along its 30 miles, needing a £250,000 police traffic post with 40 officers working eight-hour shifts. Yet it doesn't seem long since artist-poet George Harrison crossed a brook, climbed a stile, breasted fields of corn scarlet with poppies and walked under trees grown old in quiet loveliness, forming a fairy aisle of blue shadows and golden light. Wild flowers bloomed from spring to autumn, and birds were everywhere — yellowhammers, chaffinches, blue tits and a blackbird, its beak a glint of gold, shrieking discontent at George's approach. His word-picture is a memorial to the walks we once knew where now the ring road runs.

1992   TONY IRESON

The past is a foreign country.
They do things differently there.

— L. P. Hartley

LIVELY TIMES

The old-time railways stand high in everyone's affection, and it was an enjoyable trip back to the LMS in the 1920s when William Harris dropped in to tell me that he was the waiter in short jacket and bow tie at Kettering station restaurant when nobly-bearded Mr Coates presided over the busy scene with stationmasterly discipline. William started there in 1927, was a glutton for work, gained experience in the restaurant, and then graduated to the coveted job of dining car waiter on expresses between St Pancras and Bradford.

The pay was only 10s a week, but tips added £2, excellent in the twenties, and he lived on fantastic food as the travelling chef and waiters were entitled to a meal of the quality they served to the passengers, which in those days on crack expresses was luxurious. They ate at their ease in the dining car, before or after serving the passengers, whichever was more convenient: "We had the pick of the food — smoked salmon, partridges, pheasants, lobster, grouse in season, and mushrooms all the year round, which was remarkable then. The dining cars were beautifully appointed, and it was silver service with damask tablecloths.

"Passengers paid 2s 6d for the three-course lunch and the tip was usually sixpence which we handed to the head waiter for sharing out at the end of the week. He was specially interested in one gentleman I served, and wondered what the tip might be. The diner was Sir Josiah Stamp, chairman of the LMS, but he left only sixpence."

William's shift was nine hours, though he often did twelve to earn overtime. This meant starting at 7 am to serve breakfast in Kettering station restaurant, then jumping a train to St Pancras where he joined the express dining car for the working trip to

1

Bradford and back to London, finishing the day with the ride home to Kettering. Besides eating well themselves, the waiters provided drivers and firemen with eggs and bacon to fry on a shovel in the firebox; the guards were fed too, and thirsty porters at Kettering were not forgotten. Stationmaster Coates was strict, but somehow bottles of beer were regularly reported "broken" to the benefit of the porters. His refreshment was a silver service pot of coffee which had to be taken into his office exactly at 11 am, followed by a pint of beer in the restaurant at midday. To keep up to date with local news he used to drop in at the Waverley Hotel, Station Road.

Mr Coates was delighted one day. Prince Henry, Duke of Gloucester, came from London to go hunting, and as usual Mr Coates escorted him across to his carriage on the Melton Mowbray train. The Prince handed him a leather case and asked him to accept a gift as a token of his appreciation. In the case were gold cuff links bearing the Royal monogram.

William, still in his twenties, left the railway after a craftsman came to repair a sunblind on a Rothwell shop and asked him to help. William saw how the job was done, and noted approvingly that cash was paid on the nail, so ceasing to be a waiter he set up as a maker, installer and repairer of canvas sunblinds: "The first job I did was for Silver the chemist, and fitting a new blind took me a whole week, as I was learning by experience. Mr Silver seemed a bit worried, but was very understanding. He told me he had been doubtful about giving me the job as I seemed so young."

Ben Holdich became William's partner, and they built up a business as Harris Bros. of British Lane so successfuly that they acquired as regular customers William Timpsons, Marks & Spencer, Woolworths and Hepworths, fitting blinds on their London shops when needed. An incident they remembered was a daring robbery at Ushers, the High Street jewellers. Two thieves, posing as Harris employees, called at the Maypole Dairy, said they had to mend Ushers' sunblind, and borrowed a ladder. The jewellers were closed all day on Thursdays, so the men had time to lower the sunblind, nail it across the window, and shielded from view they broke in at the back, made a clean sweep, and got away.

William's publicity on his van was liable to give other drivers heart failure. A notice read: "This vehicle is being driven by a blind man." Smaller type revealed the double entendre, which somehow I don't think would pass muster in these more sensitive days.

Many aspects of railway life are described in an entrancing three-inch-thick typescript lent me by Jim Carr. In it his brother Ray, who became a Yorkshire stationmaster, surveys his life with a fine descriptive touch. Discipline in the old days could be unbelievably tough, shown when one of Ray's neighbours, a goods guard, had his lunch basket searched by railway police when he came off duty. In it they found a few pieces of kindling, left over from the guard's van stove, which the man was taking home to start the kitchen fire. Knowing that he would face a charge of theft, and feeling certain that he would lose his job and his company house, the poor chap drowned himself.

Nasty things happened when families became too familiar with the iron horse. Children played on trucks, and one girl lost her fingers between the buffers when a line of empties was suddenly shunted. A neighbour had the bright idea of using a fog signal to clear a smokey chimney, but a terrific bang and a cloud of soot betrayed his mistake. The explosion blew the oven across the kitchen. Expresses approach soundlessly if the wind is blowing towards them, as a mother found when crossing the line with her baby in his pram. As a train rushed upon them without warning, she desperately pushed the pram forwards and threw herself backwards. Both escaped by inches, but the pram freewheeled on and tipped the baby out in the gents' loo.

The Guinness Book of Records, had it existed then, would have been interested in the lightning technique of the railway tailor. Station staff needing new uniforms were lined up at the end of the platform. The tailor arrived by train to find them standing opposite his carriage door. In the briefest of halts the tailor rushed along the row of customers, recording or checking their measurements. As the train puffed out again he settled back in his seat, pocketing his notebook, rolling his tape measure, and bracing himself for another batch of lined-up customers at the next station.

Ray's station regularly sent off baskets of racing pigeons to be released at a specified time by porters hundreds of miles away so that they could fly home. On the day of a big race for a substantial prize, one of the pigeon fanciers rushed into the judges' room waving a leg ring a few seconds before the fastest bird could have returned. The ring, he said, was from his pigeon which had, just dropped into his loft, and was therefore the winner. The judges all sat in stony silence. What he did not know was that the releasing station had wired that the birds were still in their baskets because of thick fog.

A bright sunny day almost deprived us of one of our best novelists. Brother Jim — J. L. Carr, now known for his books and TV plays — then a little boy, went out for a walk. He decided to leave the path and cross a green plot at the sewage works, unaware that the grass was just a crust over deep black sludge. He fell straight through into the foul death trap, and saved himself only by a desperate struggle. The experience is still a nightmare.

Animal stories have their place. A prize cat in its basket was sent by train to compete in a show. The parcels staff could not resist having a look at it, but as soon as the lid was unfastened the cat clawed itself free and ran into a tunnel. It spurned all offers of milk and titbits and could not be recaptured. What to do? A porter had a brainwave. On the station strength were several battle scarred mouse-catching cats. He grabbed one, and sent it on to the show in the prizewinner's basket. I can imagine the comments of the bewildered judges, and the astonishment of the owner when the tattered railway cat was sent back to him. Day-old calves used to travel in sacks with only their heads showing, and kind-hearted porters would give them a drink. Poultry sent in the same way might escape and have to be captured and re-bagged as they flapped around the parcels office.

More glimpses of life in those disciplined days: While the school "crocodile" was on the march the master in charge would move along it barking out general knowledge questions and demanding instant answers. At the big house the chauffeur's daughter who worked in the kitchen answered her mistress back, and her father was ordered to make her apologise. After hearing her story he refused to side against her, and paid for his integrity by losing his job and his house. A drayman boasted of his strength and lifted enormous weights. He overdid it, strained himself and became so decrepit that his friends could no longer recognise him. In the midst of a sermon a local preacher sensed the Tay Bridge disaster and broke down, murmuring from the pulpit: "Something terrible has happened. . . ."

A lady of pleasure forced her way into the home of a railway-man while his wife was away. He tried to push her out, and in the struggle she died of heart failure. The man cut her up, and disposed of the body in pieces. His defence at his trial was that he feared his wife would find out and start asking questions.

Ray records the decline of railways after road transport started to nibble away the best goods traffic, and eventually he saw his busy station reduced to a few temporary offices. It was a long time since his boyhood when railways were the nation's arteries, and his grandfather read the Bible before meals with the family kneeling by their chairs.

Mike and Lizzie Elmore told me about their father Les Elmore, an LMS drayman, head stableman at Kettering, and later super-visory goods foreman at Hinckley. He married in 1929 on £1 1s 6d a week, which did not please his parents, as with more children coming along they needed his money. The long depression had set in, but the pubs stayed busy, and Les would still be delivering barrels of beer late on Christmas Eve. To help the hard-pressed landlords he would connect the barrels to the pumps after lowering them into the cellars, assistance acknowledged with gifts of the odd pint, a pork pie or a piece of bacon. The Prince of Wales landlord gave him a Dalmatian puppy, Paddy.

The LMS stables were behind The Crescent. They held 30 horses, were manned round the clock, and were immaculately kept. Les and Stan Hicks, his assistant, took great pride in the horses and regularly entered them in the agricultural show and hospital parade competitions with shining brasses, tinkling head bells and coloured ribbons plaited into tails and manes. To their regret they never beat the Co-op, who had so many horses that they could rest their entries the day before the parade, whereas the LMS competitors had always done a hard day's work.

Les was good with sick horses and was called on by vets to help in difficult cases. He nursed many a valuable animal back to health in the railway tackroom stall. He was one of the few draymen who could drive a pair of heavy horses in tandem, and at Kettering his skill enabled him to handle some of the heaviest loads including the girders for the Savoy when it was built.

Nervous or troublesome horses were sent from St Pancras to benefit from a quiet spell at Kettering, but this did not mean a quiet life for the drivers. One horse proved such a devil that to hold it in Les had to brace both feet against the front bar of the dray. The horse tried to kick, its hock hit the bar, and Les sustained a smashed ankle which landed him in Leicester Royal Infirmary for a year, and left him with a shortened leg. Another problem case ran away with its dray down Market Street and finished up in the portico of the Royal Hotel. Some of the decoration knocked out by the shafts is still missing.

The draymen were friends to everyone. A doctor who collected horse brasses would stop Les's dray, and if he spotted a brass he needed would take it off there and then, sending a replacement. Unusual guests, always stimulating gardeners' demands for stable manure, were the elephants whenever a circus came to town. They were accommodated with the horses, and each morning paraded past the station along Midland Road on their way to the "rec".

Mike has one fragrant memory: "Dad had his own liniment

The size and power of the railway dray horses is shown by this picture of Les Elmore with a mixed cargo at a Kettering factory. Sam, his favourite among the horses, was highly intelligent, and is wearing a fine collection of brasses on his headband and martingale. (Lizzie Elmore)

for rubbing on strained fetlocks or tendons, and because I was rather frail as a youngster he used to rub it on my arms and legs. Fine for the horses, but not for me — it stank to high heaven, and I can smell it to this day!''

An artistic flashback to the days of steam was an article in the *Railway Magazine* about Don Breckon, the railway artist who was born at Corby and attended Kettering Grammar School, where he used to sacrifice his lunch so that he could spend the hour on the station observing trains. On Saturdays he did a horse-drawn bread round to earn money to buy a bike, which enabled him to visit Cohen's scrap yard at the Cransley Furnaces site to sketch famous steam locomotives towed there for breaking-up. Art was his subject at school, he became an art teacher, moved on to full-time painting, and eventually he and his wife, also an artist, settled in Cornwall. He concentrated on painting railway subjects, and one-man shows and TV appearances were followed by books of railway pictures which have proved an outstanding success.

Around the trains he paints contemporary people, cars, buses and farm tackle, whisking the beholder back half a century and reviving the best of memories. Peter Kelly wrote: ''Don's pictures transport us to a quieter time, when families drove into the country in Austin Sevens and picnicked beside the line. As well as capturing locomotives and trains in perfect proportion and detail, his paintings come alive by beckoning us into the scene.''

The old Kettering to Cambridge single line via Thrapston has often been in the news, and two specialist books have been written about it, but I have never seen any reference to a remarkable hold-up at Christmas 1928 which makes railway history. Frank Patrick of the *Evening Telegraph*, one of the passengers involved, found out the details. At Cambridge the Kettering-bound evening train was unaccountably delayed until pressure for an explanation revealed that the railwaymen had lost the ''staff''. This was the all-important metal tablet on a wire loop which drivers had to obtain from the signalman and carry when they passed over a section of single track. They were forbidden to proceed without it, and as there was only one staff to each section, following this rule made head-on collisions impossible. The driver of a goods train collected the staff at Raunds, but found he had lost it when he reached Kimbolton.

It had fallen off the engine, and without it under Board of Trade regulations everything had to come to a standstill.

Two porters were sent off along the line with hand lamps, one from Raunds and one from Kimbolton, looking for the staff along the five-mile stretch. The Raunds man found it and walked on to meet his mate who took it back to Kimbolton, and traffic started up again. But the train from Cambridge, due at Kettering at 6.32, did not arrive until 10.25, missing all the connections.

Pictures in Book 2 of the passenger engines that worked from Kettering recalled Fred Hudson, a gifted engineer who worked for Timson, Bullock and Barber when they started business in Montagu Street, and 20 years later set up on his own. He spent 14 years making a $\frac{1}{7}$th scale model of a Midland 2-4-0. It had 7,000 parts, developed two horsepower under steam, and was used by the railway as an instructional model for training drivers. It was saved, though damaged, when Mr Hudson's workshops caught fire. Where is it now?

Dr F. Leslie Preston, whose family ran Kettering Furnaces for many years, discovered one of the little engines that hauled ironstone trains from the pits enjoying retirement in the National Trust's Industrial Railway Museum at Penrhyn Castle, Llandudno. I was sent a colour picture of the engine — Kettering Furnaces No. 3 — restored in full glory and illustrating an eye-catching handbill.

Mr Ioworth Jones, the Trust's railway engineer, told me that with members of the Industrial Locomotive Society he visited the Furnaces in the 1960s to see the fleet of steam locos busily handling the iron ore trains: ''We had some enjoyable days with the manager and engineer who showed us round. Later, hearing that the plant was to close, we asked if we could have one of the locomotives, and were invited to go and select one. We went to Kettering again, but how sadly changed we found the Furnaces. Closure was near, and all the locos had been withdrawn from service except Number 2, which was hauling out items for scrap.

''We chose Number 3, which was taken to Penrhyn and thoroughly restored as a four-year project by members of Bangor University College Railway Society. At Kettering the engine was olive green, but the students repainted it maroon with white lining, the original livery given it in 1885 by the makers, Black Hawthorn of Gateshead.''

Peter Hodson rang from Ilkeston with a story about the smallest of the engines — Number 4, nicknamed Yum-Yum. Every Sunday morning when Harry Preston was managing director of the Furnaces, chauffeur Bill Blades had to call at Avenue House (now Satra) to pick up Harry and his wife, who would be waiting in their churchgoing clothes. Bill drove them down the private road to the sidings, where waiting with steam up would be Yum-Yum, always in apple pie order with paint shining, brasswork gleaming, and her cab clean and tidy. Mrs Preston ''in frills and furbelows'' was handed up on to the footplate by her husband who then joined the driver, and the little engine puffed away across country to Thorpe Malsor. It stopped near the church for Mr and Mrs Preston to alight and stroll over to attend morning service. While they were in church the driver kept steam up ready for the return trip. It was a triumphal progress for the shining little engine each Sabbath, and because of his love for St Leonard's Church, Harry Preston is buried at Thorpe Malsor.

The car used on these occasions was the famous crimson Humber (sorry I thought it was a Renault) which Harry Preston bought from John Loake the shoe manufacturer. It had no self-starter, and the only man who could hand-swing the big engine was chauffeur Bill Blades, so that when the car changed hands he went with it to ensure its good behaviour. Harry's son Francis used to borrow the car for evening trips to country inns, but Bill was not then on duty, and at closing time half the village would turn out to push the car to get Francis started on his homeward journey. The crimson Humber with its crimson-uniformed chauffeur was a familiar sight everywhere, and when it began to age Harry was so fond of it that he had it re-bodied by Blanchflowers. Bill became Harry Johnson's driver later, and stayed with the Iron & Coal Co. until he retired.

Peter's father Tom Hodson started at the Furnaces as a boy from the Grammar School under Harry Preston, and rose to works manager under Harry Johnson. Peter joined as a trainee from school, did his National Service and then went to the Stanton Ironworks Co., but with closures in sight left the iron and steel industry for another career.

Allah Buksh, who worked at the Furnaces for a time, told me

that managing director "Massa" Johnson used to exact fines for misdemeanours. When scaffolding surrounded one of the very high chimneys a young recruit was bet half a crown that he dare not climb the ladders to the top. He set off, waved from the summit a long time later, then came down to find "Massa" waiting at the bottom. "Why did you go up there?" he asked the lad, who replied: "For a bet, and I've won 2s 6d." "You haven't," said "Massa", "I'm fining you 2s 6d for risking your neck." Among Allah's memories is the lavatory, which was similar to Army active service arrangements — a pole positioned over a trench.

Dave Lucas's terrier Scamp, which assisted the Woodland Pytchley by bolting foxes which had gone to earth, helped the Furnaces when an underground pipe between engine house and water supply became blocked, and the engineers did not know where to dig to clear it. Dave put Scamp into the pipe with a line attached to his collar, and the dog scrambled along — it is said for 300 yards — until stopped by the obstruction. He was called back and the line was paid out on the surface, revealing the site of the trouble.

Another link with the Furnaces was through Mrs Gladys Allinson who at 84 wrote from Bradford: "Kettering since 1930 has been very dear to my heart. My first job was staff midwife at the General Hospital, and in Kettering I met my husband and his family. His father was George William Allinson, a very lively member of urban and county councils, and district secretary of the National Association of Blastfurnacemen. But for illness he would have been chairman of Kettering Urban Council in 1934, the year in which he died." I was touched by her appreciative comments, especially when she said she had placed *Old Kettering* below her photograph of Mr Allinson.

As children we were fascinated by the "overhead railways" carrying customers' cash across some of the big stores. The assistant put money for a purchase into a wooden cup, clipped it on to a trolley running on a wire, pulled a handle, and it shot away to the cashier, speeding back a moment later with receipt and change. The one I knew was in Liptons in Gold Street, and Mrs McMahon of Corby (née Winifred Gleeson) remembers a similar system at Woodcocks. For anyone who wants to refresh their memory, the magazine *Evergreen* discovered one still in use in the Reminiscence Centre at Blackheath Village, London.

Winifred worked at the Co-op Clothing after leaving Stamford Road School, and helped to make suits for Bert Joyce, the KICS secretary manager and practical joker. Bert always sported a fresh buttonhole and his orders for suits specified a lapel recess for a water container for the flower. She saw the Carol Levis show at the Coliseum at which Jim Dale was one of the discoveries.

Home thoughts came from Phyllis Russell (née Steventon) of Edmonton, Canada, who was also at the Co-op Clothing: "I was overjoyed with Book 1, and still look at the pictures of the factory trying to recollect some of the faces. I started there, and have always been grateful for the training in tailoring. My two elder sisters also worked there. We were quite poor, as my father was killed in 1918. I still visit the war memorial and gaze at his name, and two years ago I went to France to look at his grave. My husband and I found it. My eldest son was with me, and it was a very moving time for us. I come to Kettering almost every year, and visit my old girl friend who lives in Warkton Lane. After 60 years I still enjoy talking of old times. My thanks for putting together a piece of history I treasure."

Winifred Spence told me that when she passes St Andrew's Church she thinks of her father, Harry Maycock, pausing there to rest on a winter's night in 1919. He had fought for two years on the Western Front, been a scantily-fed and hard-worked prisoner for 18 months, and then passed Christmas 1918 on a freezing journey across Germany in a train of open trucks, taking eight days and nights on his way back after his release. He became an influenza stretcher case in Switzerland, and was admitted to Fulham Military Hospital. He arrived at Kettering station unannounced, could find no transport, and walked home through a snowstorm.

Harry, one of Kettering's painters, was a lifelong friend of another artist and ex-prisoner, Dudley Brown. One day as they were both painting pictures of a cottage in Geddington the lady who lived in it emerged and emptied a bucket of soapy water over the pair of them. She told them that she objected to her house being scrutinised. Mr J. C. Brown, Dudley's father, like many Kettering people was an enthusiastic allotment gardener and prizewinner, and followed the custom of erecting a comfortable hut on his plot as a summer retreat. At times he was

11

wanted out of hours in connection with his leather business, and to save a messenger needlessly toiling across the allotments in search of him he flew a Union Jack on a flagstaff if he was "in residence".

Former *Kettering Guardian* reporter Ivan Smith, now in his 90s, helped as a lad on his father's allotment at the top of Pipers Hill. Access was from the bottom of St Peter's Avenue, and Ivan estimates that there were hundreds of allotments stretching down to the brook and the wall at the end of the cemetery. Alan Shearn in his reminiscences considers the allotments as valuable sources of food for families, instancing a railway porter who, with money saved by growing food and repairing the family shoes, was able to rent a large house and raise a family of seven.

Living at Elon College, North Carolina, is Old Centralian Leslie Plumb. He married Jose Mobbs, one of his school friends, and they emigrated in 1950. The 1930s books, he finds, bring back many fond memories of Kettering such as the beautiful Clydesdale horses pulling loads of coal up from the KICS depot: "I was born and raised at 77 Union Street in the shadow of S. Patrick, leather dressers, where my father was the maintenance engineer. I was the youngest of 10, am now 67, and eight of my brothers and sisters are still living. Marie the youngest daughter, blazed the trail to America after she left Rockingham Road School, emigrating in 1953 to join a pen friend. The chapter on the Central School brought tears to our eyes. It was a marvellous school and should never have been closed. Our books were brought by friends who paid us a visit — Pam and Dick Cole and Mary and Dennis Franklin. Dick, Dennis and I all played cricket for the Old Centralians."

Jose is the eldest daughter of Leslie and Ethel Mobbs, and her wedding to Leslie Plumb in 1949 was a double one, her sister Roma, also a Centralian, marrying Geoff Hanger of Plaistere & Hanger at the same time. Roma is well known in the bowls world, serving as President of the England Women's Bowling Association in 1977 when the World Bowls Tournament was held at Worthing and she was hostess to representatives from 13 countries. Les Mobbs was well known for arranging benefit matches and billiards and snooker tournaments for charity at the Conservative and Midland Band Clubs, and each year his cricket XI played a County side.

A sad day was recalled by a letter from Canon Richard Eldridge. In Book 2, I wrote of Mr Eldridge, head of Kettering Teacher Training Centre who beame assistant headmaster of Kettering Grammar School when the Bowling Green Road building was opened in 1913. Canon Eldridge wondered whether the reference was to his father. He was uncertain because when he was born in 1921 his father had become headmaster of Eye Grammar School, and during his childhood his parents never spoke of their Kettering days because of a family tragedy. His elder brother, when a little boy, had been killed in a road accident witnessed by his mother and sister.

I turned up the *Evening Telegraph* reference which showed that the accident, in 1918, happened in Silver Street when the youngster with his mother and seven-years-old sister were crossing from the pavement outside the old Wesleyan chapel. The little boy suddenly ran back — it was believed he had dropped his ball — and was struck by a lorry. Charles Wicksteed's car happened to be passing, and was used to rush him to hospital, but Dr Daniel Drake-Lee found him so badly crushed that his case was hopeless. His father and mother, Mr and Mrs F. J. P. Eldridge, who were Canon Eldridge's parents, wrote to the coroner to say that no blame was attached to the lorry driver who was travelling at only five miles an hour and stopped immediately. Canon Eldridge's last incumbency before retirement was at Belper, and wishing to move south he found a suitable house at Kettering, so returning quite by chance to his parents' former town.

Charles Wicksteed's loss of his little dog Jerry was recalled by Mrs Winnie Cox, aged 80. The dog disappeared, and despite a widespread hue and cry was never found, alive or dead. Ignorance of his fate was a permanent grief to his master, and when he was buried in London Road cemetery Jerry's lead was placed on the coffin. Mrs Cox's father-in-law was William Thomas Cox who founded the stonemasonry firm in St Peter's Avenue, and when Mr Wicksteed was planning the rose garden in the Park he gave Jerry's photograph to Mr Cox and asked for a statue of him to be made. There was fellow-feeling, as Mr Cox had lost a favourite dog out shooting, and he carved the lifelike Jerry which became such a popular feature.

Years afterwards I heard of Jerry's fate. A poacher set some

Kettering led the country in infant welfare, winning the Astor Shield for the best baby week outright in 1930. Centres were at the British School and St Philip's Hall, and two-thirds of the town's mothers took their babies to the sessions.
Here Mrs C. W. Clarke weighs prizewinning baby Margaret Elmore. *(Wilfred Elmore)*

snares near Bryn Hafod, Mr Wicksteed's home, and to his horror found the dog dead in one of them. He dare not tell anyone at the time, but later confided in a friend who told me the story, though he did not reveal the poacher's identity.

Philip Hague, who lives in Eastbourne, is a link with solicitor Frederick William Bull, author of the standard *History of Kettering* published in 1891. His father Mr G. W. Hague, worked for Mr Bull, and many of the exhibits in the old museum in the Library building were labelled in Mr Hague's copperplate writing. Remember the drawers full of butterflies and moths collected by Albert Wallis, and the remains of a Zeppelin bomb? After the war Frank Thompson spent two years restoring the collection of some thousands of specimens which were donated to Peterborough Museum and incorporated in its large lepidoptera collection, not on public view but available to students.

Mr Hague, later clerk and cashier at Lamb & Stringer, solicitors, found that his £4 a week salary allowed him to buy and run an Austin Seven, taking Philip with him when he picked it up at Longbridge. He was the last part-time secretary of the General Hospital, and for £5 a year did a similar job for Kettering Liberal Club, then a temperance establishment maintained by businessmen so that they could meet without spending too much money.

The club was the scene of one of Bert Joyce's practical jokes which backfired. A member put his new hat brim upwards on a table while he ordered a snack. This was too great a temptation for Bert, who emptied a pot of tea into the hat, ruining it. The jape delighted him until he laid a note on the counter to pay for his own tea. "Thanks — that will buy me another hat," said the victim, scooping up the money as he stalked out.

Philip Hague enjoyed circuses and fairs on the Northampton Road "rec". Bertram Mills brought Togare and his tigers, and giraffe-necked women, and paraded elephants, tigers and performers along High Street, including stilt walkers so high that they shook hands with onlookers at upstairs windows. Their enormously long trousers were made by Hepworths. At the fairs, besides stalls and roundabouts, were shows exhibiting giant rats, flea circuses, an unfortunate half-man half-woman, and a boxing booth where a bruiser took on local talent, usually headed by Art Elmore. Showman John Thurston was born in Kettering during the 1897 fair, and on his birthday which always came round when the fair was at Kettering, profits went to the hospital and children were given free rides, though I never seemed to arrive at the right time to get one. It was a happy thought to choose Thurston Drive as the name of a new road close to the "rec".

Living at 1 Kingsley Avenue and attending Park Road School, Philip had Rockingham Road Park as a happy hunting ground and learnt tree recognition there. Less peaceful than the trees were relics of World War I — two captured field guns, a tank, and a row of billets. The tank disappeared, the huts were burnt after being used as temporary housing, and the guns went to ornament Legion Crescent, one at each end beside Rothwell Road.

Bill Sellick, a wartime artilleryman, took on the job of looking after the guns. Bill, who lived at Number 12, served 15 years as a regular until his horse was hit by shrapnel and rolled on him during the Battle of Ypres. His legs were paralysed, and as a war casualty he was chosen by the British Legion to reside in one of the Crescent houses. From his wheelchair he cleaned and polished the guns and tended the gardens round them. As an old soldier he lacked nothing in determination, and when a friend fell ill he went all the way to London to see him in the wheelchair which was fitted with a micro petrol engine. It took him 24 hours steady driving to get there. One day he saw a passing tramp going through the motions of aiming and firing one of the guns and went out to protest. "See here, mate," said the tramp, "I helped to fight for these guns, and have every right to handle them. So hop it, you interfering busybody." Or words to that effect.

Ron Potter told me that kindly actions during the 1914 war continued to bear fruit long afterwards. His father and mother, William and Annie, lived at Burton Latimer, and visiting London his mother noticed Australian and New Zealand soldiers hanging about St Pancras with nowhere to go, being preyed upon by people who were after their pay. The men had crossed the world to fight in the war, and were on leave from France, but there were no arrangements for them to stay anywhere.

Mrs Potter felt that they could be found leave billets in Burton Latimer, and with the generosity of Burton people and the help of benefactors in London arrangements were made for them to stay in people's homes without charge and to receive pocket money. Ron, who was knee-high, remembers soldiers sitting at the table at home, and people going round the town with 5s each for them. When an appeal was made in 1917 for free hospitality for wounded soldiers from overseas Mrs Potter responded, and for the rest of the war men from all parts of the Empire visited Burton as guests.

She became organiser for the district, and after the war Lady Gower asked her to take on similar work for London's Winter Distress League, so that for years needy and sick children from the East End were entertained by Burton residents for holidays which lasted as long as three months if the children were ill or under-nourished. Once every three weeks Mrs Potter took 20 children back to London and collected another 20 for a spell in the country until eventually hundreds had visited Burton. "Among all the children who came to regain their health I never had a failure," Mrs Potter said.

Before the 1914 war a young single man, Dennis (Dan) Ingram worked at Cransley Furnaces and lodged with Mr and Mrs William Knight in one of the cottages beside Northampton Road.

Near the end of the war the two young Knight children, Eve and May, were playing outside when a Red Cross ambulance drew up and the driver asked for their mother. Mrs Knight came out, to find that the ambulance had brought severely-disabled Dan back to the only place he knew as home. He was gassed and shell-shocked, paralysed from the waist down, and unable to speak. With a scrap of paper and pencil he asked for a drink of water.

Warm-hearted Mrs Knight never doubted where her duty lay. She took Dan in, made a bed for him in the front downstairs room and, apart from some visits he made to a hospital at Newton Abbot, nursed him until he died in 1923. Besides looking after husband and children Mrs Knight also cared for her grandmother and grandfather in their declining years when her grandfather was suffering from facial cancer.

After Dan's death Mrs Knight determined to secure a gravestone for him, and triumphed over bureaucracy to have one erected on his grave in Cransley churchyard beside the path from the hall to the church. The inscription reads: "Pte. Alwyn Dennis Ingram, No. 31205 Royal Fusiliers 2nd Battalion, who died from the results of wounds received and of being gassed in the Great War, November 24, 1923, aged 43. This headstone is erected by his friends and the ex-Servicemen of Broughton and Cransley." I heard the story from Mrs Bernard Donnelly of Heighington, Lincoln, who in 1918 was the little girl May. Dan was thought to have no relatives, but one day a brother turned up and provided the opening chapter to his story. Dan was to have been married before the war, but opted for single life at the last moment and disappeared, coming to Northamptonshire.

For James Palmer in Edinburgh, memories of his musical family were stirred by my reference to his grandfather, also James Palmer, one of Kettering's leading musical and artistic figures in the 1930s. James went to Edinburgh by way of Kettering Grammar School, Christ's Hospital (he says C. W. Godfrey's coaching got him in), and a career as a chartered architect and town planner in London and Scotland: "I can assure you that not all of us are insensitive ogres as the Prince of Wales and sections of the media suggest."

Some of his childhood years were spent in Hallwood Road: "At Marsh's shop and market garden we bought potatoes, a penny a pound or seven pounds for sixpence in real money. Florrie, who lodged with another Marsh family, delivered milk from two big cans on her bike handlebars, and I used to imagine the disaster if she fell off. Our house, erected on a builder's yard, used left over components, and I don't think any of the windows matched. On the skyline were the elm avenues where I wandered with our dog. I remember antirrhinums growing out of the wall between Grammar School and cattle market, and the ease with which we made holes with pennies in the soft stone wall opposite Speight's.''

His grandfather James was one of 12 children born to Henry and Jane Palmer and his father Algernon (A.J.) as the eldest son trained in Ireland and Saville Row to enter the family tailoring business, but did so reluctantly as his real interest was music. He conducted Kettering Operatic Society and Wellingborough Operatic Society where he met his wife Dorothy, and as a notable cellist played under Sir Henry Wood. At one concert the soloists were Malcolm Sargent, then organist at St Mary's, Melton Mowbray, and Algernon.

Uncle John Palmer was a singer just starting with the Carl Rosa Opera Company when war broke out in 1914. In a month he was serving in France with the Honourable Artillery Company, which put paid to a music career. He joined Shell Mex and spent the rest of his life in the USA and London. Aunt Edith Palmer was known as a pianist and teacher of singing, and the musical genes also passed to James's brother John who won a scholarship to New College Choir School, Oxford, and during the last war contributed to broadcasts as a boy chorister and soloist.

The Palmers have been described as quiet men, but Tom, son of Henry of Palmers Music Stores in Dalkeith Place, became a CSM in the trenches in France, rather a change from piano tuning. Charles Palmer ran the Albion Hotel in Market Place, and his grand-daughter Mary Hanger is daughter of Tom Hale who once had a grocery business in a delightful shop between the Pavilion and the Post Office. Cousin Ralph Palmer, kindly and reserved, was organist at London Road Church and music master at Kettering Grammar School. Old boys remember him as a patient teacher who made a scratch choir sound melodious on speech day as we went Rolling Down to Rio. He allowed one of my friends to open and close his mouth, but forbade him to sing.

*Queen Mary liked to come to Northamptonshire. Here she is arriving
on a spring visit in 1938 with her hostess, the Duchess of Buccleuch.
Council chairman Walter Dyson is welcoming her, with stationmaster
W. E. Coates just behind him. Grafton and Warkton May Queens with
their retinues visited Boughton House to sing for Queen Mary.*

Soon afterwards I heard from another member of the family,
Canon David Palmer, vicar of SS Peter and Paul, Teddington,
and area dean of Hampton. He is the elder son of Thomas,
youngest of the quartet of two brothers and sisters who ran
Palmers Music Stores until it closed down. Thomas died in 1972
at 83. David's mother was Miss Lister whose highly practical
lessons on home management helped to qualify future wives and
mothers at the Central School.

He identified one of the great virtues of Kettering in the 1930s
— its stability: "Though I have always been grateful for stability
at home (just two houses and two schools) such as is truly rare
today, it took your book to analyse at a distance what a *good*
community it was in so many ways in my 1930s and through
the war. The leading figures were indeed all so stable that it was
natural for them to be philanthropic in a community they
expected to leave only at retirement or death. I was at Hawthorn
Road School and then the Grammar School (as was my father)
and remember vividly all the staff mentioned from 1942
onwards. Mr Kirby was a real friend as I became more senior."

David has been catching up on local events as he went abroad in 1974 to work as chaplain at the British embassies in Turkey and Italy.

In Rome he was in sole pastoral and administrative charge of the beautiful Anglican church of All Saints which provides a "home in Rome" for a notable mix of nationalities — residents, tourists and pilgrims — chiefly from countries of the Commonwealth, though other nations are often represented at the services. During his years there David wrote a detailed history of the church, a distinctive Victorian Gothic building erected, like St Andrew's, Kettering, to the designs of George Edmund Street, and his last commission. The history takes a wide view, including many personal stories, from the visits of members of the Royal Family when in Rome down to the remarkable feat of Mrs Pazzi, who to help the endowment fund between 1927 and 1956 (when she was over 75) made and sold pots of marmalade containing eventually over three tons (6,900 lbs). Written partly in Kettering, the book pays tribute to help from the Public Library and from Simon Thornton, who identified hallmarks on All Saints church plate. David is also a railway enthusiast, making his first observations from Panther's Field near his home in Gipsy Lane, and continuing them in many foreign countries ever since.

Two errors have turned up in Book 2. Dr William Emanuel spotted one — it was Kaiser Frederick III who died of cancer (page 103) after reigning only 99 days, and not William I. Frank Panther (page 11) became a managing director of True Form, but did not think of the name or own the shops. Name and chain were established when his business was acquired in 1913 by J. Sears & Co. Correction comes from Virginia Mackay whose grandmother Elizabeth was sister of W. T. Sears.

Finishing this chapter, I heard from Ray Carr who enclosed a page article the *Yorkshire Post* had written about him. He was for 25 years stationmaster of Stainton Dale and Hayburn Wyke on the Scarborough to Whitby Line, now closed, and by a delightful turn of fate his son Roger bought Stainton Dale station. He adapted it as his home and engineering workshops, preserving it very much as it was, including the station clock. Quite like old times is the former BR prizewinning garden, which is kept in tip-top condition and opened for charities. Ray has made a museum in one of the offices and looks after it from his house nearby.

What memories he must have as he walks through family rooms where once he ruled and regulated the busy to-and-fro of passengers and goods.

BACK TO SCHOOL

Looking back to schooldays, Pete Hanger who lives at Northampton speaks for a whole generation as we think of the masters and mistresses who strove to instil civilised ideas into the mixed bag of youngsters who formed their classes around 1930. Pete, who attended Hawthorn Road 1932-38 and Kettering Grammar 1938-42, writes: "I had the benefit of two extremely fine schools, and have great admiration for all who taught me, even those I disliked. They were dedicated, with the interests of their pupils always foremost in their hearts and minds."

At Hawthorn Road he started with Miss Jarvis's "babies", moved into Miss Dixon's class, and then on to Miss Anstey the infants' headmistress. He went into the junior school, first to Miss Woodey, then to Miss Goodman from Coventry who had just taken over from Miss Hayward, skipped Mr Moule's class to go into Miss Cawston's, and finally joined the scholarship class with Miss Butler in the school's only upstairs classroom.

"Headmaster Captain Hudson was a very proud old soldier who made sure that we observed the two minutes' silence on November 11. I remember him as 'Pop' Hudson, and though a firm disciplinarian he was well loved. He had a son, Peter, a year or two older than we were, who sometimes played football with us. He went to Wellingborough School, but I'll wager he didn't receive a better education than his father provided for us at Hawthorn Road. He went into the Army, and when I last heard of him had attained the rank of major, but he is pretty sure to have gone much higher."

Pete is right. Peter Hudson, after a distinguished career, is Lieutenant-General Sir Peter Hudson, KCB, CBE. Born in 1923, he went from Wellingborough School to Jesus College, Cambridge, was commissioned into his father's old regiment,

23

the Rifle Brigade, and commanded a company in the Mau-Mau and Malayan campaigns before taking command of the 3rd Battalion Royal Greenjackets and becoming their regimental colonel in 1968. He commanded 39 Infantry Brigade 1968-70, in 1973 became GOC Eastern District, and 1975-77 Chief of Staff Allied Forces in Northern Europe. He was Deputy Commander-in-Chief UK Land Forces 1977-80, served as Lieutenant of the Tower of London 1986-89, and became secretary-general of the Order of St John 1981-88.

Pete continues: " 'Pop' Hudson came to test us when we were in Miss Butler's class. He was quite upset when none of us could tell him the plural of 'sheep', and went down to the babies' class to get Molly Giles, six years our junior. He stood her on the table in the expectation that she could enlighten us. It would make a lovely story if she had been able to, but unfortunately she couldn't manage it. I think she became a nurse. I recall other members of staff. Mr Moule, 'Mickie' to the irreverent, a stern gentleman and the only teacher I knew who came to school by car, Mr Payne who came by bus from Corby, and Mr Lawnden the caretaker.''

He lists some of his classmates: "Stan Mobb, my best man in 1954; his second daughter qualified as a pharmacist like myself. Terry Wright, a tall centre-half, scored a memorable goal that must have given Pele ideas, and became mayor of Kettering. Olive Watts became mayoress of Northampton. Bob Coleman qualified as a librarian and when last I heard of him was working in New York. Geoff Langham had a beautiful soprano voice and sang 'O for the Wings of a Dove' at speech day. Velma Simmons and Don Needham married each other. Fred Barrett, a smashing inside right, came from Burnley and returned there. Stuart Shrive, a stocky lad one year younger than the rest of us, farms at Brigstock. Sheila Cheney became a leading light in Kettering Operatic Society and starred in *The Lisbon Story*. Bernard Wright, son of the famous 'W.B.' went to Stamford Road and Wellingborough School, becoming a director of Frames Tours. Two sets of twins were Joan and Barbara Caswell and Joan and Kathleen Skinner. Duggie Underwood, a nippy outside right, became a Bevin boy and moved to Nottingham. Vic Clarke moved to Corby, and others I remember were Joyce Goodall, Terry Asher, Mavis West, John Wesson, Colin Tite, Jean White,

'Nip' Collier, Dorothy Loasby, Fred Eady and Hazel Wareing.

"Was Mrs Beryl White in Book 2 formerly Beryl Ogden? If so she was a classmate of mine, a tall, friendly, happy girl. Of course, in those days we were not interested in girls as such. That came when they separated us after the eleven plus, and was, I have always maintained, the reason they parted the sexes."

At the Grammar School in September 1938 he found that nine of the 11 masters in the 1928 group in Book 2 were still there. Mr Gash (art) had been replaced by Mr Cork, and Mr Hum (junior science) by Mr Gladden. Additional masters were Mr Coates (Latin) and Mr Smith, a pleasant Lancastrian (Latin, English and Maths). Mr Coates took their first Latin lesson, and one bright spark obviously primed asked what was the Latin for "the". As there is no equivalent, the question flummoxed the young teacher and the class burst out laughing, but he joined in the amusement and all was well.

Pete found that H. E. Bates was right in one respect about headmaster J. I. Scott — "He didn't need much excuse to cane you, but I never held it against him. Even at 14 I realised that the officer must support his NCOs. I liked some of the masters better than others. I detested 'Weeky' Wood, didn't like Godfrey one little bit, and 'Tinny' Tynan wasn't much better. 'Dodger' Whitney, nicknamed after a Rushden pugilist, was serious and well-meaning, but often couldn't get his experiments to work, and would say 'Well, you'll just have to take my word for it.' I always think of him when his successor Mr Perry the satellite tracker is mentioned. I had great respect for 'Bennie' Woodward, EEK (as Kirby signed himself), and 'Pecker' Hopkins. I had a friend John Garley who was good at French but not at maths, so we came to an arrangement whereby he did my French home-work and I did his maths. Mr Tynan suspected nothing, but Mr Hopkins marked my work 0 out of 10 with the comment 'I've marked this work before in Garley's book.' He said nothing to either of us which was very astute. Just think of the caning we'd have received from JIS if this had been reported to him. John Garley became an actor, was Joe the Milkman in the BBC's first soap opera The Groves, and married June Brown (Dot Cotton of EastEnders), but sadly died in his mid-thirties.

"In September 1939 'Sergeant' Coates and 'Reggie' Gladden went to the war, and we did not return to the school until October because the air raid shelters were not completed. Then we attended only for an hour and a half on three mornings a week, virtually to be given homework. In November we began a regime of 8.30 am to 12.50 pm Monday to Saturday, and homework continued very heavy. The High School also attended in the mornings, and in the afternoons the Grammar School half of the building was taken over by the evacuated South West London Technical College, while similarly the High School side housed the Dame Alice Owen School from London. When I left in 1942, JIS seemed in good health and there was no hint of illness or retirement.''

Don Sinclair sent many memories from Bury St Edmunds. Like Margaret Whiteley he enjoyed his time at the Central School (1932-36) and was a contemporary of her sister Mary who was tragically killed near Rushton a few years ago. His progress to the Central School was through Stamford Road under Miss Campling and then Mr House until reorganisation took him to Park Road where his class mistress was Miss Wills and the head was Mr Partridge. ''I took to the Central School like a duck to water, and my affection for it continues to this day. It seemed a big happy family with great staff/pupil relationships, a high standard of teaching, and masters and mistresses who gave much of their time to a wide range of activities out of school hours.

''Bill Steer and 'Panty' Braithwaite managed the school soccer teams (East and West), and Miss Latcham and Miss Morgan ran the girls' netball and hockey teams, assisted by Miss Everett, the delicious art mistress whose charm was not lost upon the boys. Miss Morgan and Mr Matthew helped with the League of Nations group, Miss Latcham and Miss Ralph with the drama group, and Mr Bell in his woodwork room organised the production of props for extra-mural enterprises, including many for the all-England school sports on the town cricket ground in 1935. Mr Steer, and later Mr Braithwate, were scoutmasters for the school troop, and Miss Latcham was mistress of the guides. Mr Silby, Mr Steer and Miss Morgan managed the boys' and girls' athletic teams.

''The Centralians dance band formed by Mr Braithwaite in the early 1930s was always popular, playing for enjoyable parties at the school and dances at the Central Hall on Saturday evenings, but folded when members were called up in 1939 and 1940, and it was a pity it was never reactivated. The 1930s were a successful sporting era for the school, and one could be proud to be part of it. I played for Central East, though not regularly as I had very good contemporaries — Dud (Ginger) Sawford from Twywell, Fred Draper, Ray Panther, Arthur Sellers, Geoff Simcoe, Norman Mutton, Dennis Watts, Bob (Lanky) Johnson a super goalkeeper, and Ewan Marlow are some who come to mind. In Central West I recall Gus Margetts, Norman Kemp, Paul Curtis, Pete Lansberry, Harry Sawford (Dud's cousin who perished in the war), Basil Brooks and Reg Collins.

"The cricket team's success in competitions was assisted by the practice net in the playground. 'Nogger' Claypole from Stoke Albany hit three balls in succession over the school building, and 'Dobbin' Smith could pitch his bowling on the length spot painted on the ground five times out of six. Others I think of are John King, an elegant opening bat who later played for Kettering, Paul Curtis, a hard-hitting opener, and Fred Roughton, a steady bowler later with Perfecta in the town league. Founder members in 1938 of the Old Centralians XI which played in the town league until a few years ago were Arthur Sellers (captain), Dennis Watts and Bill Brooks (opening bowlers), Arthur Barringer, Norman Mutton and 'Lanky' Johnson (wicket-keeper). 'Panty' Braithwaite was always around with the Old Boys team, as being a Yorkshireman he was a cricket fanatic.

"Our swimming team, usually managed by Bill Steer, regularly won the cup at Fineshade Abbey Lake. Strong swimmers were Derek Rideout, Len Hudson and Ray Jones (all later swam for Kettering), Gordon Jones, Ray Panther and Dennis Watts. We were encouraged to learn to swim at the weekly baths session, and many of us obtained the Royal Life Saving Society's bronze award.

"Some quite talented performers represented the school in town events and Kettering in schools county athletics. Among victor ludorum winners were Dennis Barber, Fred Draper whose younger brother Bill played for Kettering, and Gus Margetts, a good all-rounder now in South Africa, with Ray Panther and Dennis Watts who also went to South Africa as strong contenders for the honour."

Don's friend of schooldays and for many years afterwards was Edward (Ted) Barnes Sismore who lived in Neale Avenue and went into the borough council treasurer's department. When war broke out he joined the RAF, in which he was destined for a remarkable career and daring exploits that thrilled the nation during dark days. He became a navigator and bomb aimer, and in 1941 survived an operational tour in Blenheims when the attrition rate was high. Transferring to Mosquitos he took part in many low-level daylight raids. In 1943 as a pilot officer he gained the DFC in the first day raid on Berlin, acting as navigator to the leader and dropping the first bomb. The raid compelled Goering to abandon a broadcast and take refuge in a deep shelter. Later that year as a flying officer, Ted was awarded the DSO for his part in the raid on the Zeiss works at Jena. He gained a bar to his DFC for outstanding work as navigator in the leading aircraft of a large formation which attacked the Gestapo headquarters at Copenhagen in 1945, and a second bar when he flew with great distinction against a similar target at Odense. Broadcasting later, crews of following aircraft said that his aim was so accurate that one bomb went through the front door of the Gestapo HQ. He stayed in the RAF after the war with a permanent commission, and gained the Air Empire Medal as navigator for breaking the out-and-home record to the Cape in 1947. Later he received the Air Force Cross, awarded for peacetime acts of gallantry.

Don recalls that in 1950, seeking new worlds to conquer, Ted persuaded the Air Ministry to allow him to train as a pilot and go on to fly jet fighters, which he did so successfuly that eventually he had his own Javelin squadron at Leeming. He did a spell in Germany as a station commander, and retired in 1976 as an air commodore to live a country life near Maldon, Essex. Don too was a pilot, getting his wings in 1942 and serving five years with the RAF, partly as a flying instructor.

He has happy memories of Mr Walpole, the school caretaker nicknamed ''the Colonel'' who acted as referee and umpire and spent a lot of his free time coaching the boys in athletics on the Grafton Street field. He held sessions in the boiler room with a blackboard to mastermind goalscoring strategy. Don always looked him up on return visits.

Caning was an occasional observance. Headmaster Iwan Russell used one when unduly provoked, always in his study. Mr Braithwaite caned boys but never girls. He gave victims a choice — one whack with the cane or write out 50 long words,

28

increased when necessary up to 300 words or six whacks. He was nonplussed when one of the girls, possibly Joan Haynes, opted for whacks instead of words, but solved the problem by letting her off for showing pluck. Bill Steer kept a size 10 slipper, used to good effect on boys only. Miss Morgan had a cane, but never used it.

Many High School girls came from out of town, and some who travelled by train indulged in pranks which luckily did not get to the ears of Miss Whyte, the headmistress. One lively spirit was Rosalie, daughter of Rev. Henry Newton, minister of Wellingborough Baptist Tabernacle. A man passenger seemed to be asleep and the top of his coat lay unbuttoned. The girls industriously filled the space around his neck with orange peel. When they got out at Kettering the sleeper winked at Rosalie, evidently having enjoyed the game as much as the jokers.

Rosalie became a missionary in Spain, was caught in the fighting when the Civil War began and was brought out of danger by a British destroyer. She attended theological college, then joined a woman missionary who had her own compound in northern Nigeria, reached by voyaging up the Niger. They were independent of any society and lived by faith, trusting that their needs would be met by friends. They worked in many ways for the native community, and several orphan babies were thrust upon them, one arriving on the doorstep in a basin. They named him Peter, and brought him up to be a splendid Christian worker, receiving theological training in England and returning to start a college, only to lose his life in a road accident. Rosalie's colleague died too when she rose one day to greet the dawn.

Left alone, she created a centre for teaching, retreats and conferences, attracting Nigerian Christians from a wide area. She became a living legend — a lone white woman living in her spacious compound with bungalows for guests amid lawns and flowering trees, lovingly tended by a native helper who stayed with her for 30 years. Rosalie brought together Nigerians who formed a trust to carry on her work, and they took over when she died in 1988 aged over 80. "My heart is in Africa," she said, and she lies buried in the compound beside her two friends. Her brother David Newton of Stamford told me the story. David Dulley the Wellingborough brewer was a Baptist pioneer, and the chapel and manse where David and Rosalie spent their childhood were built by William Dulley about 1870. In 1900 a later David Dulley put the land and buildings in trust for the Strict Baptists in perpetuity. Dulleys closed in 1920 along with many small breweries making distinctive local beers.

Rosalie left her compound to the care of Nigerian friends who hope to make it a centre for medical work named the Miss Newton Memorial Hospital.

Jim Dodge has many schoolday recollections. "Avondale Road infants was a one-storey building in white stucco behind tall railings. Its playing fields lay wide and green. Mum entered me when I was four. It was, I realise now, a very advanced school. In the babies' class we had a sand tray and made patterns and structures with wooden rods and cubes. We had our afternoon sleep on camp beds in the hall, or sitting at tables with heads on folded arms when we moved up. The headmistress was Miss Campling, a lady with black hair who wore blue frocks with white collars.

"We were taught to read by phonetic methods, and arithmetic started with an abacus. We said our prayers and sang a hymn in the hall every morning. When Lady Alice Montagu-Douglas-Scott married the Duke of Gloucester we stood with our mothers in Stamford Road, waving paper Union Jacks as they were driven past to Boughton House. For George V's silver jubilee we each received a mug and a silver badge and had a whole day's holiday, but had to go into school to drink our one-third-pint bottles of milk.

"When it was time to move to a junior school we were entered at St Mary's. The headmaster, Mr Shepherdson, was a tall, stooping man with greying sandy hair and a cultured voice. Our first teacher, Miss Hodson, a lady with shingled fair hair, caned us on the hand for talking, boys and girls alike. Her room reverberated to the chanting of the alphabet and multiplication tables. She had to convert us from pencils to ink. Two girls, the ink monitors, fetched trays of inkpots from the cupboard and brought them round for placing in the holes on top of the desks. We sat with arms folded while the monitors circulated again with bottles and filled the inkpots. Miss Hodson counted out steel nibs and told us she would want them back at the end of the lesson, though we could keep the wooden holders in our desks.

"We fitted the nibs and were instructed to suck them for

several minutes, dip them in the ink and stroke away the excess on the lip of the inkpot. Then we wrote an exercise in our lined books until Miss Hodson told us to stop. The monitors brought pink pen-wipers, the nibs were collected, and Miss Hodson counted them back into their box. The same ritual continued daily until we were judged fluent writers. Farewell to Miss Hodson came with promotion, either to Miss Brunsden who took the slower children, or to Miss Rees.

"We found Miss Rees as noisy as we'd expected, having heard her through the partition, but not nearly so fearsome. She was dark and plumpish, rattled us through hands-up mental arithmetic every morning, and introduced us to long division, multiplication of pounds, shillings and pence, and rods, poles and perches, and the twin pinnacles of eleven and twelve times tables. It was usually in arithmetic that she lost her temper, but she never pointed at any particular child, and once we realised that we could almost enjoy her fulminating for its histrionic appeal. We liked her and she seemed to like us.

"Miss Rees was a dedicated royalist and imperialist. On Empire Day, after Mr Shepherdson had recited poetry about this sceptred isle, she unrolled a map of the world and advised us to be proud that a quarter of it was red. She showed us how the English, Scottish and Irish crosses fitted together to form the Union Jack. She produced a picture of General Gordon at Khartoum surrounded by dervishes and said he was a true Christian gentleman. She used pictures in history lessons, pinning them round the room. She had Bruce and the spider, King Charles in ringlets and a lace collar looking through the branches on Oak Apple Day, a fort on Hadrian's Wall when she told us about the Roman roads, naval heroes Hawkins, Drake and Frobisher, and Captain Cook being clubbed to death. She unrolled a bit of the Bayeux tapestry showing Harold with an arrow in his eye. Cromwell she ignored, but Charles I was pale and dignified on the scaffold. She had King John looking embarrassed at Runnymede, Nelson dying and reminding us that England would expect us to do our duty, Florence Nightingale, and Eric the Red in a longship bursting with round shields and horned helmets.

"Each Monday morning Father Cooper or Father Knight came to lead prayers and keep us up with the ecclesiastical calendar, and Father Cooper told us he had been a boxer before he became too heavy. On saints' days Mr Shepherdson read an appropriate story leading up to martyrdom. Though the school was Anglican, it had a pronounced strain of medieval English paganism. Miss Rees taught us country dancing and had us circling the room in mixed pairs as she played the Cornish Floral Dance on the piano. At the bazaar the maypole and St George and the Dragon were central attractions. The most impressive dragon had a green tail made from a stocking, and a cardboard head like a crocodile through which he puffed talcum powder smoke from a football bladder. Everybody clapped as he steered down the yard towards St George, and the action proceeded in a series of scuffles and shouts, ending with St George's foot on the dragon's neck. The saint's armour was made of cardboard painted silver-grey, and he wore a chorister's cotta with a red cross tacked on to it. His helmet, made by Mr Simms, had a visor that opened and closed.

"Mr Simms bulked large in church and school affairs. He ran the football team which played in white shorts and blue and white shirts with lace-up necks. As St Mary's had no playing field we practised on Mill Road 'rec' or Miss Butcher's Bible Class field. In 1939 we won the town junior schools league but lost the cup final when I was first reserve. We got gold medals for winning the league, and bronze ones for losing the cup.

"Many things about Mr Simms' class aroused our envy. It contained the oldest and toughest boys who had benches along the walls, a wood-turning lathe and a gas ring for boiling glue. They were allowed to use Winsor & Newton colours out of tubes, and the walls were covered with their pictures of tanks and fighter planes. On the bench were models of aircraft with propellors powered by twisted elastic, and fretworked Spanish galleons, their parchment sails decorated with Maltese crosses. Centrepiece was a half-completed model of Nelson's *Victory* on which they worked in groups from detailed plans, and they were going to do the *Cutty Sark* next. We went in once a week, but only to paint, and look.

"Our envy lessened, though it never disappeared when we heard that Mr Simms' class were not to take the annual schools examination, and we were. The exam was to select for the Central, High and Grammar Schools, and comprised an intelligence test for which we practised with Mr Shepherdson and sat before Easter, followed by a whole day being tested in mental arithmetic, and composition. Scholarships, free places, or half-fee places were awarded, the first two worth the same, but a scholarship carried more distinction. The Grammar School also had its own entrance test.

"Mum told me that if I was to go to the Grammar School I must obtain a free place. I didn't see this as a threat — it was simply a fact. We knew children on the estate who had won scholarships but had not been allowed by their parents to take them up. They would have had to agree to stay at school until 16 instead of leaving at 14, getting a job and taking wages home. Mum's concern was not a desire for money — just simple awareness of the lack of it.

"I got my free place. Three of us went to the Grammar or High that year, and there were only seven children from our estate in the two schools. Mum got me to wear my new badged cap two weeks before the autumn term started, and was laughed at in Edgar Road." Jim, who pays warm tribute to both Scott headmasters — JI and AF — was one of the 1939 KGS intake from which the sixth form of about 15 sent eight members to Cambridge and two to Oxford. Cambridge claimed Chris Griggs, John Kirkup, David Barlow, Geoff Ashman, Michael Williamson, Gordon Hulett, Peter Paul Tomlinson and Jim Dodge. Eric Colville and Bill Asbrey went to Oxford. Jim's brother John followed to Cambridge a couple of years later with Eric Leadbetter, a rugby blue. Also memorable was Bob Baker who traversed along the exterior stone cornice that runs round the Bowling Green Road building at top-floor level. He was invited to leave, and became a paratrooper.

Jim Dodge became headmaster of Lutterworth Grammar School 1962-84, while John went on from the *Evening Telegraph* to work with Reuters and hold public relations jobs, eventually becoming director of the National Council for Training Journalists and the UK's first professor of journalism at the City University. Jim read the lesson at his brother's memorial service at St Bride's, the Fleet Street church. John's death at 54 was a sad blow.

Roy Goodfellow was the original drummer in the Central School dance band when it was formed by Mr Braithwaite the maths master. Roy had a musical background, for his mother Elsie (née Middleton) was in silent film days the pianist in the

33

Victoria Picture House orchestra, and played at the Pavilion and Empire. At the Vic mice used to run over her feet while she was playing, attracted by popcorns dropped by the audience. Roy made his first public appearance at 11, on drums for his mother when she gave a concert at the Midland Band Club.

The Central School band played for weekly dances at the school, and at 15 Roy dropped a clanger. He went to the Melton Arms for a pint during the interval, was late back, and dancing had resumed without him. "Your services are no longer required," was Mr Braithwaite's frosty greeting. Roy joined Charlie Walker's band, earning 5s a night increased to 7s 6d if they played after 11 pm. He remembers Dr Flack as a caner because when the knobs broke off his drumsticks the headmaster took them to add to his armoury of canes.

Roy worked for Booth Horrocks and for Phonotas the telephone hygiene firm, playing in the evenings with Tom Ashby's Rhythm Aces. The band broke up when war came, Roy went into the RASC as a driver, and had a pleasant surprise when musicians were ordered to fall out. They were taken to a room where stood Private ("Babbling Brook") Donald Peers. "I'm your new boss, boys," he told them. He formed a band with himself as leader, and they played for the troops all over Western Command until preparations started for the Second Front, when they rejoined their units. Roy landed with the invasion, went through to Germany and was wounded. He belongs to the Normandy Veterans' Association.

After the war he returned to the Rhythm Aces, re-formed as the Modernaires after Tom died. The band was one of the best in the district, winning a *Melody Maker* contest at Northampton Salon de Danse when Roy took the award for best drummer. Many people knew him as a fitter for the gas board and one of their top appliance salesmen. One of his memories is typical of old Kettering. His mother used to invite people in for a musical evening, including instrumentalists and such powerful singers as Frank Evans and Horace Lansberry. Outside, a crowd gathering to listen would block the pavement in Regent Street.

Roy's wife Dorothy knows most Kettering people of her generation. She was on the sweet counter at Woolworths, the busiest in the store with bags at 2d and 4d a quarter. There was no leaning on the counter, even for a moment, as the sweets cash flow was relied on to keep the store takings on an upward curve. Charlie Curtis the manager, a byword for efficiency, would stand at the top of the stairs, letting his eagle eye roam round, and there was nothing he missed.

When Ted Grove was Centralians' drummer the band was engaged for many big occasions such as the Burns Night and St David's Night balls and the NALGO and GPO socials. Centralians, from autumn to spring for several years until 1939, held a public dance every three weeks, and Mr Braithwaite as band manager was meticulous in his selections, timing them so accurately that each programme always ended on the dot. Similar organisation marked the regular dances at the Central School. Admission at 1s was by being known to the doorkeepers, or introduction by someone known to them. Names of new dancers and their sponsors were recorded in a book.

Allah Buksh lent me some copies of *The Grammarian*, magazine of Kettering Grammar School when it was in the now-demolished Gold Street building. They cover 1902 to 1908 with three issues a year, largely preoccupied with football and cricket, but giving glimpses of a scholastic life that set a high standard.

Headmaster J. H. Gill had succeeded Thomas Widdowson who had lost pupils through his insistence on a classical education. Gill restored the numbers from a handful to almost the capacity of the building by introducing a modern syllabus and was so popular that the boys clubbed together to give him birthday presents including gold sleeve links, an expensive set of chessmen, a travelling clock and a leather dressing case. In return he entertained the boys, their sisters and girls from Miss Butcher's High School to a luscious Christmas tea. He was a good cricketer playing for the school against such opponents as Kettering Thursday, Market Harborough GS, Parents XI, the Post Office and Whitfield Hodgson & Brough, easily topping the batting averages and pulling many games out of the fire, so that in 1908 KGS won 11 of its 12 fixtures.

The school staged ambitious theatricals, hiring the 900-seater Victoria Hall next door for an annual two-part production in which the boys presented the first half, and then the staff took over. At Easter 1905 over 500 people attended to see the boys give *Vice Versa* and the staff present a second play called

Freezing a Mother-in-Law. Other activities included drill, inspected by an army officer, swimming, and ambitious cycling outings, one of which took the boys and their bikes by train to Sheffield whence they set off on a 60-mile Derbyshire tour taking in Bakewell, Haddon Hall and Chatsworth before returning to Sheffield and catching an express home.

Boys familiar later as leading citizens figured in unusual roles. Vincent Mobbs appeared in a play as a young lady, wearing a golden wig, and wrote for the magazine an account of a stay in Germany. Herbert Winterhalder became a professional footballer, was outside-left for Sheffield, and the whole school went to see him play when the Cutlers lost 2-1 to Kettering in 1902. T. N. Bird when an old boy captained a scratch football team which threw down challenges to the school. F. W. Goodwin threw the cricket ball 53 yards, a record until beaten by T. Mansbridge with 59 yards. F. W. Goodfellow was hailed as a great acquisition to school football. Joe Baker left to go to Bridlington GS and escaped unhurt when a fall of cliff killed a master and two boys with whom he was walking. Sons of a Parisian family named Thiebaud came as boarders. W. J. Thompson passed the Institute of Chartered Accountants prelim exam in which Latin was compulsory. Alfred East, at the height of his success, lectured to the school on Japan. Long illnesses were rife, five boys missing the whole of a term. In a viva-voce those who answered every question were W. H. Tailby, R. D. Tozer, C. F. Seddon, L. V. Everard, C. J. Seddon and R. F. Watson. Mr F. Peet, science master, took a tough holiday aboard a trawler off Iceland in rough weather. H. R. Goosey, E. A. Goosey and W. Lewis won prizes for maps of Europe. Max Depensier, a boarder who had been in England only 2½ months, gave the best recitation at the school concert. At midsummer 1903 Mr Gill was displeased by poor attendance. It was Feast Week.

A boy who spanned the generations was Bernard Pledger, an all-rounder who got 100% in the Latin exam, captained the football and cricket teams and bagged prizes on speech day. He left in 1906, became a master at Kings School, Gloucester, and during the 1939 war returned to KGS, teaching Latin. He proposed the toast of the School at the 1947 Old Boys' dinner.

Philip Hague fills in interesting facts about Park Road infants

36

In this 1931-2 group of Park Road boys, Phil Hague is front row right, and to the best of his recollection others in the picture are, back row, left to right: 1, 2, 3, Arthur Pentelow, Gordon Seer, Mervyn Owen, and John Draper at the end; middle row: 1, 2, Peter Kilsby and Billy Collis, 4, 5, Norman Blunsom and Ronnie Beeby; front row: 2, 3, Gordon Foster and Cyril Pettit, 6, Len West, 8, Bob Kilsby.

and junior schools which have happy associations for people who spent their childhood in the north end of Kettering. Miss Spinney, the infants headmistress, had charge of Philip when he started: "Some pupils were a bit frightened of her, but she had a heart of gold. She loved the children, and many loved her. Any doubters should have seen the string of little boys and girls who held on to her hands as she walked to school from her Kingsley Avenue home. She grew four chestnut seedlings in pots on her study windowsill, planted them in the playground, and they became the trees beside the wall bordering Park Avenue." Miss Maddison was his first class teacher — one of the sisters who used to play chamber music as the Maddison Trio.

He had a special connection with Park Road as his mother, Ada Hague (née Beard) had been on the staff before the 1914 war, teaching infants as she had the Froebel qualification. One of her favourite pupils was Pat Thornton, the future jeweller: "He was so well-mannered and kind, and used to draw wonderful pictures." When she went back to Park Road in the early 1930s after her marriage she had in her class a five-year-old who always understood things first time, and she felt sure he would be successful in life. He was Barrie Chambers, future graduate, Parliamentary candidate and mayor. Ada was with Miss Spinney during her last three months, then under Miss Hurst and Miss Dixon, and during the 1939 war spent her last teaching years at Henry Gotch. In Park Road junior, with Mr Partridge as headmaster, Philip was in Miss Cunliffe's class, and then with Miss Wills who was responsible for scholarship work: "Only eight scholarships to the Grammar or High Schools were awarded each year, and Park Road always seemed to get the lion's share." Other mistresses included Miss Fairie and Miss Wagstaff.

At the Grammar School Philip was taught Latin by headmaster J. I. Scott. Latin was not the form's best subject, and at the end of the fifth year Mr Scott set an exam. Weeks elapsed, but no results were forthcoming. At length one boy had the temerity to inquire. Mr Scott, after a pause, replied: "They are the most disgraceful papers I have ever seen. No one, apart from Derek Gray, has more than 30 out of 100, and Collins received only one mark." Ken Collins, pushing his luck, asked how he had earned 1%. "For spelling your name right," came the sharp rejoinder. Obviously this was a milder JIS than in my day, ten years earlier. "I think he was unwell, and had lost the fire you knew," says Philip. "It was 1938, and he had not so very long to live." (Collins' 1% was outdone by David Barlow the musician who failed to get any marks at all in a maths exam set by Mr Hopkins.)

One of Philip's contemporaries was Roland Tomkins, a brilliant pianist who became Roland Shaw the arranger and band leader, and another was John Clifford Ireson, a future professor who Philip says was reckoned by JIS to be the most brilliant boy ever to pass through his school. Another obvious candidate for the honour, H. E. Bates, had then blotted his copybook with JIS, but after the old headmaster's death both were paraded in double harness as star speakers at important events such as the retirement dinner of E. E. Kirby in 1950. Cliff occupied a chair in French at Hull University, retired in 1982 with the title of emeritus professor, and went to live at Tours.

In the same age group was Keith Panter whose father kept the Melton Arms. He was always in trouble, and as an insurance against caning wore a square of leather in the seat of his pants. He joined the RAF and flew with distinction during the war, gaining the DSO as a flying officer for gallantry during a raid on Germany. With his plane ablaze, he dragged his trapped navigator clear, and both bailed out. He stayed in the RAF after the war, and pioneered air-sea rescue.

Among masters who live on for Philip are Mr Woodward for his uproarious rugger concerts, Mr Kirby who said he would be content if he could get every pupil for the rest of his life to look up in the dictionary any word he did not know, and Mr Gladden who predicted that one day everywhere would be artificially lit and we would so crave for occasional gloom that we would carry ''darks'' — torches that would produce darkness.

More about J. I. Scott's free use of the cane came from John Knight of Walgrave. When his brother Leslie was at school a deputation went to the head to complain about some difference with their form master. JI opened his door, and without listening to them commented: ''You have appealed to Caesar, and shall receive Caesar's judgement.'' He reached for his cane, told each to bend over in turn, and administered six of the best.

A good many schoolboys and girls worked in their spare time on paper rounds or jobs in family businesses. Ben Reynolds at 14 attended the Grammar School during the week, and on Saturdays was in charge of transport from the family foundry at Little Harrowden, delivering castings to customers in Wellingborough and Northampton by horse and cart. The day started when Ben fed and harnessed the horse, putting its collar on upside down and then turning it round, bending the tail hairs back on themselves to get them through the crupper, putting on the saddle and bellyband, placing the bit and bridle, backing the horse into the cart and threading the reins through the harness rings. Starting was by flicking the reins, stopping was with a ''Whoa'' and a gentle pull on the bit. The horse was left unattended while Ben went in to see customers and arrange the unloading. Good training for a schoolboy.

The few cars and motorbikes were fascinating objects. The sturdy workhorse for some years was the Model T Ford, priced at £110, and one of the first signs of between-wars affluence. Nicknamed the ''Tin Lizzie'', it seems to have faded into history unloved, though it was an extraordinary and unconventional vehicle. Ben, who drove one, recalls that there was no gear lever and no accelerator. The engine speed was set by a hand control on the steering column, and a handbrake lever and three pedals were the remaining controls. Pressing the left-hand pedal started off the car in first gear, and lifting the foot off engaged top gear — there were only two forward speeds. The right-hand pedal was the footbrake, and the middle one reverse. There was a self-starter, but often hand starting was necessary, and the car could be temperamental, with the 23-horsepower engine capable of giving a hefty kick. If the engine refused to start, jacking one rear wheel off the ground and cranking with the transmission engaged and acting as flywheel usually persuaded it. Henry Ford said customers could have the car in any colour they liked so long as it was black, which may have been one reason why nobody seems to have mourned the old "Lizzie". A yellow one would have been irresistible.

Fred Moore remembers when he and his aunt, then aged seven and 11 and attending Rockingham Road School, used to go with a hand truck to George Wright's factory in Tresham Street. They picked up leather pieces and took them to Fred's grandma in Duke Street. She was a clicker, and with patterns and clicking knife cut out small decorative parts for shoes. The children returned them to the factory at the end of the week and picked up grandma's pay, which varied between 2½d and 3d a gross. Tiny pieces of left-over leather fuelled the copper to heat water for washday, and for the family's weekly baths before the kitchen fire. They took turns in a tin bath, using the same water topped up with jugfuls of hot.

Harold Dilley as a boy hand-barrowed all the pigswill from the Royal and George hotels along the High Street to his grand-father's pigsties at the bottom of Lower Street, making two journeys for 4d a week. His grandfather, Thomas Preedy, was well known as a pig breeder. This was an extra, as Harold's main spare time job was helping Mr West the Dryden Street newsagent. He got up at 4 am, collected national papers from the station, sorted them and before school made deliveries to customers between St Peters and Kingsley Avenues. After school he delivered copies of the *Evening Telegraph* until 7 pm. His paper round wage was 4s a week.

Alan Shearn's thoughts on old Kettering after a professional life elsewhere gave a perceptive summing-up: "The 1930s school buildings were pleasant to look at. They are still much the same, more likeable than recent teaching factories of concrete and plate glass. Educationally they deserve respect. Most children when leaving were fluent in reading and writing and had enough general knowledge to equip them for most jobs. Those who went to the Central School were fitted for good positions in offices or for training in skilled crafts, and from the Grammar and High Schools many qualified for university or a profession.

"My experience was that at every level teachers showed sincere understanding of pupils. Usually discipline was strict, but seldom unfair. Corporal punishment was so rare that fear of the cane was more frightening than the physical pain when sometimes the worst happened. The most unpleasant aspect of the elementary schools was in toilets and classrooms. The closets were invariably at a distant part of the playground and nearly always filthy. Cloakroom pegs were so close together that the clean clothes of one child were in contact with the dirty ones of another. Wash basins of heavy brown earthenware became more repulsive when teachers sent pupils to wash inkpots in them. In all other respects I think the schools compared favourably with those of today."

TECHNICOLOUR BOULEVARDS

For many people the street in which they were brought up arouses as much affection in retrospect as does their town. David Bradshaw feels this as he looks back on Russell Street, home to his family for three generations, where he spent his childhood and youth, met his wife, and lived at the beginning of their married life. "I genuinely believed as a child that the world revolved around Russell Street. I bored all my aunts and uncles to death by insisting that whatever their address, even if it was on the fancy new Naseby Road council estate, it was hopelessly inferior to mine, at Number 81, slap bang in the centre of my technicolour boulevard, itself the centre of attraction in Kettering. Russell Street was my Times Square, my Piccadilly Circus, my Broadway. All life's rich patterns were there. It was my boast that anything you could get anywhere else you could get in Russell Street."

David, now press officer at Butlin's, Skegness, certainly lived with diversity. To begin with, the Coliseum theatre, later the Savoy with its blazing technicolour sign, was just across the road. His grandmother, Mary Elizabeth Bradshaw, provided "digs" for the artistes as did other families in gaslit three-bedroom terrace houses without bathrooms, indoor toilets or hot water. Many of the theatre folk were foreign, which meant that Mrs Bradshaw had to keep a register of aliens, adding to the glamour.

His playmate was Clarence Scouse at Number 67 whose father, a former AA patrolman, worked at Bagshaws Motors in Tanners Lane. This meant that after Sunday School at Toller the youngsters had a wonderful playground among disused lorries and buses kept for spares in a vehicle graveyard. Another connection with motors was through the Orsborn family, to

43

David almost like the street's royalty, seeming to have riches beyond the dreams of avarice. They occupied shops at the Gladstone Street and Gordon Street corners, known as the top shop and the bottom shop, and their garages and transport premises were next to the theatre. It was said that proprietor Robert Lewis Orsborn, known as Pop, and his matriarchal wife Grandma had been in service as butler and maid but left their jobs to set up as carriers with a handcart, graduated to horses, and so to lorries and buses.

Their daughter Bessie married Billy Brackwell, and with their children Arnold and Edna they lived with Pop and Grandma at the top shop, a newsagents which sold a variety of other goods. The family were staunch Conservatives — Pop was a councillor — and they hoisted a blue flag during elections. Another daughter Nellie never married, was liked by everyone, became the street's "auntie", and when Grandma died inherited the bottom shop. Son Bert drove the lorries and buses which Billy Brackwell kept in repair, and among David's happy memories are trips he, Arnold and Clarence made with Uncle Bert to "help" him with deliveries. They went every Saturday and every day in school holidays, visiting Northampton, Wellingborough and Leicester, so that David saw plenty of the country at an early age.

Besides the magical theatre, Russell Street possessed Kettering's Fred Astaire, namely Reg Civil, tap dancer extraordinaire, who owned a dancing school, toured professionally, and seemed likely to leave for Hollywood any day. He lived with his grandma, Mrs Essam, who owned a beautiful black and white cat, Peter, which she assured the children was originally Dick Whittington's cat and accompanied him to London. Reg joined Arthur Remington in a double act called Nelson and Drake, and a similar partnership was formed by Arthur Turner who lived at Number 57 and fellow singer Will Sykes, the pair touring the clubs as Arthur and Will. Arthur was a leading pianist and teacher of music and singing who supplemented his income by proof reading at the *Evening Telegraph*.

David had the best of all reasons to remember "Russell Street's own dance venue Kingsthorpe Hall, provided by Mr Miles the Newland Street fish merchant who lived at the street's most distinguished privately-built house. He erected the hall as a meeting place for the street and as a dancing school for his beautiful and talented daughter Mary, who in her teens and twenties was an object of admiration in her very latest new-look fashions.

"At a social evening at Kingsthorpe Hall I met a rather self-assured exciting and talented girl, Norma Cheney, who with the professional name of Mona was well-known locally as a soubrette. Once when she was jokingly telling me what to do I remember defending myself with the comment: 'We're not married yet, you know.' But we were a few years later, in 1952, and have been happily content ever since, still in love and unlikely ever to be separated by anyone other than the Great Reaper himself. We lived in two small bedrooms with my parents before moving to Market Harborough, and undoubtedly the similarity of our backgrounds and beginnings has been the foundation of our marital success.

"Above Kingsthorpe Hall was a confectionery shop like no other, owned by the Misses E. and J. Hammond. They sold sweets and chocolates unobtainable elsewhere in the town, and unaffordable by most Russell Street residents. They were said to have their windows dressed professionally three times a year by someone from London, and their fortunes were founded on the proximity of theatreland a few yards below, for who could think of going to a film or a show without a bag of something special?

"Other shops were on the York Road corner, at the bottom owned by Mrs Sears and later Mr and Mrs Fox, and Blackwells opposite Orsborns' Gordon Street shop. There were more shops around and under Kingsthorpe Hall including Tommy Pickford's for fish and chips, George Brown's for fireworks, cycle and radio shops, and Mr Baker the cobbler, respected as the father of a trumpet player who emerged from dance bands to become the world-famous Kenny Baker of the Kenny Baker Dozen jazz band. Almost next door to Reg Civil, Dick Fox's dark green window proclaimed him a turf accountant. From lucky bags to cycle lamps, from biscuits and eggs to bed clothes and pegs, the Russell Street shops seemed to sell everything."

David remembers welcome and friendly street traders too. Mr Clarke came on Tuesdays with fresh vegetables on a cart drawn by his horse Phyllis, for whom David always saved the end crust of their loaf. Mr Watson came on Thursdays, also with vegetables, hoping the customers had not spent all their money with Mr Clarke, and the fish man came on Fridays with his wares in a big wicker basket. On Fridays too the butcher boy from Parkers in Sheep Street called for orders. During the last war he was taken prisoner, and a letter he wrote to David's mother about his experiences made her cry.

Mr Binley came with bread on Mondays, his assistant accepting a cup of tea which he drank from the saucer to save time in cooling. Mr Newne played a barrel organ to which David sang 'In the Valley of the Moon', but Mr Newne was blind, didn't realise he was a little boy, and used to address him as Daisy. Billy Hallaway from Geddington brought fresh milk in a churn polished like a mirror, and after serving the customary pint filled David's baby mug for him free. Lewis Halbard who became a councillor was also a daily visitor with the Co-op milk cart. His mare was very popular as she regularly unburdened herself between David's house and Number 69, home of Mr Yates, and it was a race to see who could scoop up the steaming heap for the back garden.

There was plenty of work, though not at high wages, in retailing, the boot and shoe trade, and Job Lee's engineering works and forge. Colin Ball went there at 14 for 6s a week and was allowed 1s of it for himself. When David, impressed, asked how he would spend it, he said "6d pictures, 3d hair cream, and 3d sweets." Colin loved animals but was never allowed to have any. He wanted to be a vet, and used to talk to Harry Blades, an assistant to Trevor Spencer in St Peter's Avenue. Most Russell Street residents were too poor to take their animals to a proper vet, so it was to Harry with his layman's knowledge that they turned. David reflects:

"We seemed to have it all. It appeared surprising that people did not wish to stay for ever in Russell Street. They could have done — there was a perfectly good hotel called the Avenue with stables where Jack Slow, lifelong chauffeur to Mr Gravestock whose shoe factory was also in Russell Street, kept his employer's magnificent Humber. Mr Gravestock bequeathed it to Jack, who ran it as a taxi. T. N. Bird also had a factory in the street, which later had Dolcis emblazoned across it."

After long and varied experience he sums up life in the 1930s: "It was a time when no one needed to go much further than their own front door in search of help, company or advice; when neighbours gossiped over garden walls or gathered in the street to talk on summer nights. Housewives nourished a determined rivalry to have the cleanest steps and windows, but generally it was a time of sharing and experiencing together such pleasures as life afforded. Incomes and expectations were low, but generosity and tolerance were high. Rights were seldom invoked, but responsibilities were actively sought.

"Looking back on those impoverished, struggling, sometimes horrendous yet halcyon days, I realise that my Russell Street was not the oasis of bliss and hub of vitality I believed it to be. But it was a microcosm of life, my home, my childhood fairyland, my technicolour boulevard, and the fiery furnace in which my character and personality were roughly forged. And I am all the better for it."

Jim Dodge lived at 12 Althorpe Place ("the Square") on the Stamford Road council estate. His memories of personalities are pin-sharp too, but as his surroundings were open he could take part in street games which were not suited to older and busier areas. Games followed a strict seasonal pattern set by the girls: "A fathomless intuition told them when catty had to give way to marbles and when the whip and top season began. Tops were either 'jam jars' which were hard to get going but stable when spinning, or 'window breakers' which were mushroom-shaped and striped red and white. A good whip would project them for yards to come down spinning, but they needed the smooth surface and width of a road."

Girls and boys played catty together, picking sides. Catty and stick were made from a broom handle, the catty six inches long and sharpened at both ends, and the stick 18 inches long. To play, the catty was placed over a hole or leaned against the kerb, and with the stick the player looped it up and away, clouting it on in mid-air if he could. When it landed he was allowed three goes at tapping the pointed end, and when it sprang in the air hitting it with the stick to knock it on as far as possible.

"Accomplished players could keep the catty in the air by juggling it with the stick, and each time they hit it they doubled

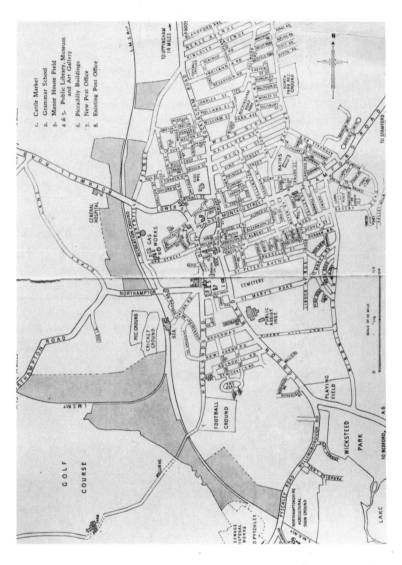

Exiles demanded a map of 1930s Kettering. This, from a Burrows guide, shows how compact the town was. The General Hospital stood almost alone beyond the railway to the west, and eastwards the Council estate and the "Poet" roads had only just crossed the Windmill Avenue – Avondale – Bath Road line. Blandford Avenue and Pytchley Road were the north-south limits.

48

or trebled the final score, which was calculated by measuring the distance from the start in foot lengths. If the catty went over a hedge you scored 100 and out and had to go and find it.''

Catty holes were rounded and enlarged for marbles. Girls played with clays at 2d a bag, but boys favoured the knocking rules with more expensive glass glarnies, the smallest and cheapest 1d for five. Clear ones with coloured stripes in them were superseded in the 1930s by semi-opaque versions with broad internal whorls. Playing knockers along the gutter coming home from school you might lose a fortune in glarnies if you had underestimated your opponent.

Hopscotch tended to be a girl's game, and in season the pavements and some roads (even Hawthorn Road, for example) were turned into numbered squares to be one- and two-footed out and back. Though most of the boys could skip like boxers, skipping was a girls' game, in time to such chants as ''Pease pudden hot, pease pudden cold, pease pudden in the pot, nine days old'', or ''My mother told me, I never should, play with the gipsies, in the wood.'' Piggy-in-the-middle was for girls, and they kept it to themselves. Facing one another, two would throw the ball to and fro over the head of a challenger standing between them. She would leap for the ball, and when she intercepted it change places with the thrower. Queenie was a game in which the sexes mixed. Whoever was ''it'' stood on one kerb with his back to the others on the opposite kerb. He threw a ball backwards over his shoulder without looking, waited for the call ''Queenie'' and then turned round to guess from his rivals' expressions who was concealing the ball, changing places when his detective powers met with success.

In games needing a challenger, picking the first player to be ''it'' was by drawing the shortest twig or reciting ''Eeny-meeny-miny-mo, catch a nigger by his toe, if he hollers, let him go, eeny-meeny-miny-mo,'' touching one person in a ring at each syllable and selecting the one touched at the end of the jingle. This innocent rhyme would no doubt be considered racist now.

High Cockalorum was too rough for girls. One side lined up at right angles to a wall, bending over head to tail. The other side, strongest first, ran up and took a flying leapfrog jump in turn, trying to land astride as far as possible along the row of bent backs. The sides changed over at the end of each attempt, or if anyone fell off, scoring according to the number of players able to achieve a seat. By contrast five-stones and flicking cigarette cards were quiet games between pairs of children. Five-stones, needing considerable skill, entailed tossing the stones up and catching them on the back of the hand. Flat stones could be bought in boxes at five a penny, but spherical jacks in the sets were unsuitable so that two boxes were needed to get five stones. Jim found suitable ones in the garden.

Cigarette cards, nicknamed fotes and begged from grown-ups, were currency for a special week each summer: "When the Fair arrived at the end of June, fote-a-go developed in imitation of the fairground stalls. Out came dart and bagatelle boards, skittles, home-made hoopla rings and spinning arrows. You paid in cigarette cards so that at the end of the day you might have completed one of your sets."

Boys with old pram wheels would make soap box trolleys. Two pairs of wheels were attached to a plank, the front ones pivoted and steered with a loop of rope. A seat made of a box with a folded cloth to cushion against splinters was fixed, and volunteer pushers were enlisted as motive power. Racing was downhill or round a block and speeds attained were consistent with nasty grazes and damage to clothes when spills occurred, despite braking with a wooden lever which pressed on the pavement.

Interest in outdoor games ebbed as the nights drew in. Some youngsters hedge-hopped from garden to garden knocking on doors and running away, or fixing a button on a long cotton to tap on a window. Mildly amusing was leaving a watch or coin on a lighted path so that some unwary grown-up would bend to pick it up, only to see it whisked away on a length of black thread by hidden and giggling jokers.

At last came the autumn game of Release: "A street lamp was the focal-point. Two sides were picked, and the hunters counted up to 100 and shouted 'Coming' before pursuing the hunted in the darkness. To take a prisoner you held him by one arm and tapped him on the head, bottom, and the small of the back with the formula 'Head, tail, bedlam'. Thus disabled, the captive was led to the lamp post, to stand touching it until the end of the game or until he was released by a fellow team member getting through the cordon of hunters to tap the post with a finger.

"Despite the chill of autumn evenings it was a game that could go on for hours, sometimes for several nights, as the only possible end was to have all the hunted captured and gathered under the lamp," Jim says. "It was usually started by one or two of us walking down the Square and up the friendly bit of Naseby Road (some of it was hostile) shouting 'Release', then waiting for shadowy forms to slip out of the darkness and into a lamp post's circle of light.

"On fortunate nights there would be a watchman sitting by a hole in the road. They were usually oldish, bad tempered, and otherwise unemployed. Sometimes ours would let us sit by his brazier and roast small potatoes, but inevitably we would irritate him and he would lose patience and tell us to clear off. Then from a safe distance we would sing 'Dan, Dan, the dirty old man, washed his face in a frying pan, combed his hair with the leg of a chair, Dan, Dan, the dirty old man.' There were dull times when yodelling round the Square enticed nobody out to play, but they were few, and it never seemed long before something interesting happened."

Summer and winter, as bedtime approached, mothers appeared calling the children home: " 'Time to come in' was first uttered more in hope than expectation. Then louder, and more threateningly, 'I said, time to come in.' It was a point of honour not to respond at first, but you would at 'If you don't come in this instant I'll tell your father to get his strap to you,' which merited a token clip of the ear as you went up the path. To be dragged in physically after all else failed was the mark of a leader whose fate would be the subject of speculation that night and inquiry the next day."

When Jim and his brother John went to St Mary's School they got to know Fuller Street, its 300 yards linking Mill Road and Stamford Road. On one side the facade of houses between a sweet shop and a junk yard was unbroken except by entries, but on the other side were St Mary's School, a short terrace, St Mary's Church, and the solid wooden gates of the slaughterhouse behind Bosworth & Bedford's butchers shop: "We never sought the place out, since it aroused mixed fascination and guilty disgust, but it was compulsively unpassable, and if the slaughterman was kindly disposed he would let you watch him stun a bullock or slit a pig's throat. In late afternoon on killing

51

days, blood, sawdust and disinfectant were brushed across the pavement and into the gutter."

Jim was a connoisseur of sweet shop goodies: "Mrs Clarke who kept the shop seemed very old, dressed in black, and stood very still in the corner behind the counter. She sold nothing but vegetables, sweets, and a few apples and oranges, largely depending on the schoolchildren. At the back of each window were rows of jars on shelves, and the sweets in them were dispensed in ha'porths — black or white striped bullseyes, red and yellow peardrops, light and dark striped mints, gobstoppers, giant humbugs, chocolate drops, mint lumps, mintoes, everlasters, treacle drops, candy sticks, liquorice torpedoes, jelly babies, Mynard's squares, wine gums, jellied fruit, clear mints, Victory V lozenges, sugared almonds, mixed rock, dolly mixtures, mint imperials, Palm toffee, chocolate-coated raisins, aniseed balls, sherbert and liquorice root. Also in the window were trays and boxes of Cadbury's dairy milk chocolate. Bournville plain, Fry's chocolate cream, wine gums, marzipan teacakes, and toffee still in the trays in which it had set, waiting to be broken up with a hammer.

"A large box contained the liquorice assortment — shiny Spanish sticks, whirls of tape round aniseed balls, imitation pipes with hundreds-and-thousands for glowing tobacco, red and black bootlaces in hanks, and miniature walking sticks. There were unshelled monkey nuts, lucky bags containing five toffees and a disappointing bauble, and chewing nuts.

"We eyed all this through the window, and rang the brass bell on its spring as we opened the door. Mrs Clarke in her carpet slippers walked to whichever bottle or box we indicated, and with a small shovel transferred the sweets to the scales, on which the ounce weight spent most of its time. In summer she sold home-made and custardy ice cream, but we depended more on the 'Stop me and buy one' men selling wafers and cornets from trikes.

"We had a Saturday penny to spend and a Wednesday half-penny. Mum would sometimes give us a penny for a bag of chips between us, either from the Mill Road dripping shop that could be smelt a mile away, or from Cornwall Road. The shop in Bath Road served ha'porths, and let you have batter bits for nothing. Dad occasionally gave us a halfpenny, and a Saturday morning spent putting Silvo on everything in the cutlery box fetched a penny. Visiting aunts usually left a halfpenny for each of us. Since the better-quality sweets were twopence a quarter and others threehalfpence, the halfpenny was our standard sum for spending in a single transaction. The penny was a measure of some extravagance.''

Jim's description of catty is expanded by Dr E. C. Bate Smith of Cambridge who left in his memoirs of Kettering a description of an earlier version which he knew as tip-cat and considered to be derived from the ancient game of knur-and-spell. Under his rules the player began by striking the ''cat'' on one of its points, and when it jumped in the air propelled it as far as he could with a swinging blow. The score was measured in foot lengths, after which the striker laid down his stick at the starting point. One of the other players then threw back the ''cat'', and if it hit the stick the striker was out and his score did not count.

From St Albans, Miss Mary Clements, formerly of Brewery House off Gold Street, describes the game Statues which used to cause a good deal of commotion at its height: ''Two people would face each other and hold right hands at arm's length, then pull each other round fast. When they had become giddy they had to release hands, stagger away, and 'freeze' in whatever ridiculous attitude they eventually finished up, to the amusement of everyone watching.''

Backstreet games in those days could be played without danger from fast traffic for Jim Dodge saw only one regular caller at Althorpe Place who did not come by muscle power, either of legs or horses. This was the doctor, and even he left his car in Naseby Road and walked up, carrying his black bag: ''Carts, drays and vans brought the coal, milk and bread, and collected the ashes. Horsedrawn too were the rag-and-bone cart, the roadmending tar boiler, and the hearse. Those who came by bicycle were the milkman, telegram boys, the knife grinder whose pedals also worked his grindstone, the window cleaner with his ladder on his shoulder, and the district nurse.

''The postman came on foot, pushing his red wickerwork parcels truck, and Mr Pettit the pedlar, in flat cap and a long brown overcoat, pushed a deep wooden box on bicycle wheels. He opened it to display reels of cotton, packets of pins and needles, darning wool, shirt buttons, shoelaces and Cherry

Blossom boot polish, all in shelves and boxes under the lid. In the well of the box were packets of tea and sugar, Camp coffee and HP Sauce, dusters, dishcloths and Beechams powders. A wooden tray which he lifted out and placed on the handles contained nothing priced at more than a halfpenny. There were sweet-cigarettes, thin bars of toffee, sticks of liquorice, liquorice bootlaces, twisted barley sugar sticks, little boxes of violet cachous, dolly mixtures, miniature liquorice allsorts, bubble gum and Wrigley's spearmint.

"Every Saturday we watched from the living room for his cap, seeming to slide along the top of Bellamy's hedge. All the children ran out to meet him, and he never served anyone out of turn. After our halfpennies and pennies had clinked into his tin our mothers came out for cottons and pins and other items they'd fogotten to put on the Co-op order.

'When everyone had done, he'd slowly close his truck, light his short silver-lidded pipe, and pass beyond our ken for another week. We spent two-thirds of our pocket-money with Mr Pettit, and never dreamed of doing otherwise."

In those well-ordered 1930s days the steam roller was the only power-driven vehicle seen in Althorpe Place until one day Corona deliveries were made by lorry and one of the residents bought a Morgan three-wheeler which he kept in his garden under a tarpaulin, heralding the motor age.

MOTHER'S WEEK

Women worked in the Kettering shoe factories before marriage, and sometimes on shorter hours after they married, but in the main they assented to a strict division of labour. It was the husband's job to earn a living for himself, wife and family, and the wife's duty was to look after her husband, rear the children, and care for the house.

Jim Dodge sums it up precisely: "If you had a chap your duty was to feed him. You knew that, and he expected it. The men took the unquestioned view that their function was to bring in the wages, and the women's part was to see that they were in a fit state to do so. They didn't expect their wives to work in the factories, but they considered their own contribution to be paramount, and the women's to be naturally subservient to it. Though the wives might question it among themselves, they broadly accepted their place. You heard often of men who threw their dinner at their wives, but rarely of any wives who threw it back."

Sid Dodge, Jim's father, came from Leicester where his father managed a small shoe factory, but they fell on less prosperous times and, at Kettering, Sid left school at 13 to work at Easts. Early in the 1914 war he was in France, held back by an eye defect but serving at the front with the RAMC. He came home to work at Birds as a rough-rounder, a heavy job performed standing and positioning each part-made shoe in a machine which drove in heavy nails round the seat, fixing together sole, upper, stiffener, lining and insole and then shearing off surplus sole leather. It was a tiring, monotonous job which Sid performed from 7.30 to 5.30 each weekday with an hour for his midday meal, and from 7.30 to 12.30 on Saturdays, getting one week's holiday a year.

The job was so tiring that when he came home in the evening and sat in his high-back Windsor chair to put his slippers on, he would sometimes fall asleep before he could get to the table for his tea. Jim says: "He was entitled to be tired, yet it never seemed to occur to him that Mum worked a longer, harder day. He simply took her for granted most of the time, and she slipped into the lives of her children."

Away from the factory, Sid always seemed to be doing something. He kept the garden going, built a shed, maintained the bikes, mended the footwear, and could if pressed make a pair of shoes. He was gifted as a singer and actor, and filled secondary principal parts in the Operatic Society productions. Thursday was always his private practice night at home, and the family would hear him singing all the good old songs besides his parts in the operas, ranging through such favourites as *The Student Prince, Rio Rita, The Maid of the Mountains* and *The Vagabond King*. For the youngsters his songs brought into the house the language of poetry.

To Jim, Dad's work in the factory necessarily remained mysterious, but he closely observed his mother's tasks at home, recorded in the fullest detail which I can only precis in the hope that one day he may donate the full version to the Public Library reference room.

She liked the family to call her Mum at home, and so Mum's day began soon after six o'clock when she cut and packed Dad's sandwiches and filled his flask of tea for his ten-minute break in the middle of the morning. They breakfasted on porridge together, and Dad went off on his bike at 7.20. Mum roused the children and gave them breakfast, in winter porridge with golden syrup and cold milk, and in summer the cereal Force (on the packet, High o'er the fence leaps Sunny Jim, Force is the food that raises him). Maybe there would also be bread and jam, bread and dripping, or bread and lard with salt and pepper. Then Mum would pack lunches of bread and butter and Marie biscuits for them to take to school.

Every day, except for occasional Saturdays, she cooked a large hot dinner which on weekdays had to be ready on the dot of 12.45 when Dad came home from the factory with only half an hour in which to eat it before going back. Apart from the meal, each day had its special character and allotted tasks, beginning with Monday when the family wash had to be done by hand. The convenience of today, when a machine can do the whole wash without anyone even putting a hand in the water would have seemed like a glimpse of heaven to anyone faced with a 1930s weekly wash.

Jim well remembers the dreaded routine. On Sunday evening his father filled the gas copper, and first thing on Monday his mother lit the copper, got his father off to work, then took up the kitchen coco-matting and pulled out the dolly tub and tin bath. Gas was a blessing — many families had to kindle a coal fire under their copper in the small hours. Breakfast over, Mum soaked badly-soiled clothes in cold water in the sink, filled the dolly tub with hot water from the copper by carrying it in the tin bath, added a blizzard of soap flakes, and put in the first lot of washing. She replenished the copper for boiling whites and heavily soiled things like Dad's working smocks, then started dolly-pegging.

Only those who have done this know what hard work it was. The heavy dolly was like a milkmaid's five-legged wooden stool with a sturdy shaft rising from its centre and a two-handed cross-piece about waist high. Seizing the cross-piece, the operator had to plunge the legs into the tub and twist the dolly violently around and back, working up a lather, swirling the clothes, and persuading the dirt out of them. Jim says: "When Mum's endurance was waning, she'd ask us to help. You took hold of the handle, thrust down and turned, raised and turned, raised and turned and raised and turned, each time with a downward thrust *ad infinitum*. The soaking clothes resisted, and if you lost the rhythm twined themselves round the legs of the dolly. Your arms ached, then your back, and then your legs. I remember dolly-pegging and pitching barley sheaves as my two most exhausting activities."

Shirt collars, the crotches of long pants and combinations and tea stains on tablecloths were rubbed with hard green soap, and bulky things when boiled were so hot that the dolly tub had to be dragged to the copper for them to be lifted from one to the other on a copper stick. Some rinsing was done in the tub, some in the sink, hot and cold water being carried again and again. Loose wringing was by hand, and the heavy damp clothes were piled in the tin bath ready for mangling.

Halfway through, Dad with the youngsters came in for dinner, finding the kitchen full of steam, the window clouded up, and the floor swimming with soapy water. Dinner, scrambled together between dolly-pegging and rinsing, would be cold mutton from Sunday, bubble-and-squeak left-overs, and cold jam tart. There was tension in the air, for Mum was tired, but she might smile and let the boys finish the mangling. By afternoon she liked to have the whites soaking in the sink with Reckitt's Blue bag, and Robin Starch mixed and ready.

Jim admired the magnificent mangle: "Five feet high, on cast iron supports, it stood firmly on the quarry tiled floor. At the top was a screw handle for increasing the pressure of the wooden rollers which were a yard across and eight inches in diameter. With your right hand you gripped the handle on the heavy flywheel and turned, driving the rollers through big iron gear wheels which Dad kept lubricated with vaseline. You fed the wet clothes between the rollers, folded them thicker and put them through again until the last drops of water trickled out and into the tub underneath. Then, carried in a wicker basket, the clothes were hung on the garden line, secured with pegs bought from the gipsies. It was a matter of honour to get sheets billowing in the breeze as soon after dinner as one could."

By dark all the washing came in, transferred to a clothes horse before the Triplex stove, or in winter hung along the top of the fireguard. A disaster that could happen was the collapse of the line on a windy day. Muddied things just had to be done again. Finishing off meant bucketing out the dolly tub and mopping the floor so that it dried before teatime when Dad came home, expecting to find everything in order and his tea ready. With Mum exhausted, this was the low point of the week as she ended the day sitting quietly by the fire and drifting into sleep.

Tuesday was dedicated to ironing, but not until afternoon because in the morning Mum biked to Barton Seagrave to do two hours' cleaning for a lady in a big house. This, with the Co-op dividend, produced the only money regarded as her own. Dinner, prepared after she returned, was fish, and then the kitchen table was cleared for ironing, Two flat irons had been heating on the gas rings, and taking the first one Mum tested the temperature by spitting on it, then tried the iron on a sheet of brown paper before running it over the clothes with a sweeping and softly thumping motion. On sheets she'd flick a sprinkling of water ahead of the iron, which hissed as it slid along. When cool it went back on its ring and the freshly-heated one replaced it.

Wednesday was difficult for food, especially if there was nothing from Sunday left in the meat safe. Mum did not care for offal such as pigs' trotters, chitterlings or calf's heel, though Dad liked black pudding and Mum used tripe in her treatment for pleurisy. Pig's liver and steak and kidney was as far as she went, so Wednesday dinners tended to be scrag end of mutton, toad-in-the-hole, stewing beef or steak and kidney pudding with a chewy lid of sweet dough.

On Thursday, Mum again went to Barton, and dinner was similar to Wednesday but more sparing as there was less likely to be much left from Sunday. Friday, like Tuesday, Mum treated as a fast day. Dinner was fish, brought daily in ice from Grimsby by rail, collected from the station by the fishmongers before daylight, and cheap besides being fresh. Often there would be grilled young herring with chips and tomato ketchup, hake or halibut poached in milk, or smoked haddock steamed in milk between a plate and a saucepan lid and served with mashed potatoes. Plaice seemed expensive, but as a treat Dad would occasionally be given one for tea covered in yellow breadcrumbs and darkly crisp at the edges.

On Saturdays Mum almost took a holiday, serving faggots and fried peas when Dad came home from his morning's work. In the afternoon they went down to the market and bought fish and chips, or a quarter of ham, or a half of haslet, or pink and yellow Russian slices for tea, which Dad might supplement with hot salted peanuts from Woolworths. Sometimes the family would call at the Co-op and Labour Institute for tea and iced buns before buying fish and chips and chasing home to eat them warm. Dad went to the club later, and Mum and the youngsters had the wireless to themselves until it was time for cups of cocoa or Oxo and bed.

Sundays were splendidly different. Mum and Dad had a lie-in (except once a month when Mum went to Communion), they all had breakfast of bacon, egg and fried bread together (a whole egg for Dad and half one each for Mum and the youngsters), then the children went to church, Dad set off on his bike to the club or some of the village pubs, and Mum was left alone to cook Sunday dinner. This would be a good cut of mutton, or sometimes lamb, beef or pork, roasted with baked batter pudding.

There would be lots of gravy, and potatoes mashed with butter and milk to a floury stiffness, carrots, kidney beans grown by Dad and bottled if out of season, and garden or dried peas. Sometimes there would be a boiling fowl with big potatoes cut in half lengthwise, all crisp and dripping-tasting, and at harvest time rabbits were cheap and were roasted and stuffed with forcemeat, followed by lemon curd and jam tarts.

Tea on Sundays was special. First came sandwiches of tinned red salmon, sardine and vinegar paste, or chopped hard-boiled egg and salad cream, all of which had to be eaten before they could pass on to tinned sliced peaches or pineapple cubes with dairy cream, sliced bananas in custard or jelly trifle and blancmange, all with bread and butter, and to finish off, one of Mum's Victoria sponge sandwiches. Supper was baked pudding and cocoa.

Jim says: "It's hard to know how we ever did anything but eat on Sundays. It was like a weekly mardi gras before six days of Lent, and must have made more than a dent in Mum's housekeeping although it provided for Monday and perhaps for Wednesday, when she could clamp the mincer to the kitchen table and feed it with scraps of meat and potatoes for mince tart or Cornish pasties." Sunday left the family with full bellies to face Monday's washday, and suet dough more than anything filled them for the rest of the week. Favourite fillers were bread pudding with soft chips of suet and sultanas, bread and butter pudding, roly poly with currants or jam, rice pudding, steamed sponge, treacle pudding or treacle tart, with rhubarb, raspberries, apples and bottled pears and plums.

Mum sang about the house and read Grimm to the children, besides having a great stock of stories of her own. She loved flowers, and grew pansies, pinks, London pride, nasturtiums and night scented stocks, Michaelmas daisies and hollyhocks. She pointed out lords and ladies in the ditches, cowslips, lady's bedstraw and smellsmock. She loved conversation and the Communion service, and three years before she died Jim found her holding her own with a group of Cambridge dons: "When she sang 'The Mistletoe Bough' at Christmas she could make us see Lord Lovell's daughter in her wedding dress, and hear the chest snap shut.''

The life of the house sprang from Mum, who had the laughing openness of a girl, overlaid yet not destroyed by sadness and determination bred of difficult experience. She was never idle unless she was ill, and rarely then. Jim says she talked and sang and played with the children, knitted knickers, vests, jumpers, socks, scarves and pullovers, and as an accomplished seamstress from her time at the Co-op factory, where she started at 13, made most of her own outer clothes and things for the boys, though their Sunday suits were made by Mr Griggs who worked as a tailor from his front room in Mill Road. Jim remembers his mother's German treadle sewing machine as the most distinguished piece of furniture in the living room.

The health of the family was maintained by Mum. For bowel regularity, everyone took two cascara tablets every Friday evening, and other remedies were Ex-Lax, syrup of figs and senna pods, with castor oil as the ultimate resort. Her other specifics included boracic powder or iodine for cuts and bumps, Sloan's liniment for aches, and cod liver oil and malt to keep colds away. If a cold developed, hot water and lemon and a spoonful of Owbridge's were prescribed, and if it got worse the sufferer, under a towel, had to inhale the vapour from hot water and menthol crystals, and afterwards go to bed with flannel smeared with wintergreen on the chest. Zubes or lumps of butter rolled in sugar were for bad throats, Vaseline would cure cold sores and stop Wellingtons from chafing, and Snowfire ointment eased chilblains and chapped hands.

Hot-ache from snowballing she would deal with by blowing on small hands and tucking them into her armpits. Septic cuts or boils needed a hot bread poultice, stys were lanced with a darning needle sterilised in a gas flame, and splinters were lifted out with a needle. Everyday washing was done in the kitchen sink where Dad shaved every evening. Mum washed after the family had left in the morning, behind the net curtain with the back door locked. The family bathed once a week, the children on Friday night, in the ground floor bathroom which contained the iron bath on crocodile's feet, the copper gas geyser, and a slatted wooden drying stand, but no handbasin. The lavatory was next door, just as draughty as the bathroom, and as these were downstairs each bedroom was equipped with a basin, ewer, and jerry in case of illness.

"Mum was very serious about teeth. Dad kept his own until the day he died, but she lost hers at 40. She made us brush our teeth twice a day, using Gibbs Dentifrice, and insisted that we brushed up and down and not across. She turned the Demon Decay adverts into a story, and did her best to wean us off sweets. Treatment for illness too serious for home remedies was provided for by paying subscriptions to the union sick club, the Windmill WMC sick club, and the Free Foresters, so that all the family were panel patients. There were plenty of doctors who looked after their panel patients and waited for their fees, becoming local folk heroes and 'real gentlemen' in a way that factory owners couldn't get within a mile of. Nevertheless, you only sent for the doctor or went to sit in his waiting room as a last resort."

Superstitions were heeded if not seriously entertained. Palms were checked to see that lifelines had no breaks, help me to salt meant help me to sorrow, you avoided walking under a ladder, swallowing orange pips caused appendicitis, two teaspoons in a saucer presaged twins, being born in a caul was lucky, tree or bush foliage was banned in the house except at Christmas, a double crown and money spiders were signs of wealth, while unlucky portents were whistling indoors, seeing the new moon through glass, putting boots on the table, and breaking a mirror, so earning seven luckless years. Spilling the salt was unlucky if you neglected to throw a pinch over your shoulder, putting on a garment inside out was lucky if you left it so, and being bombed by a bird was lucky if you did not clean off the mess. Good omens were having a black cat cross your path, and seeing a penny and picking it up. Crossed knives pointed to a sudden end and were hastily uncrossed, while a crow was watched to see which house it marked for death. A single magpie was a bad omen only cancelled by seeing another, you never stepped on cracked paving stones, always crossed over to avoid one-legged men, and believed swallowed hairs twined fatally round your heart. People spat on their hands to seal a bargain, crossed fingers warded off all evils, and the shouted formula "King-its" would prevent an enemy doing further damage during a fight. On the first of the month you could pinch and punch, shouting "white rabbit" to prevent retaliation. Sticking a stamp on upside down was treason and illegal, and you did no washing on New Year's Day in case somebody died.

Though everyone was frightened of consumption and scarlet fever, death in reality did not loom large. It seemed remote, just a matter of drawn curtains and men pausing to remove their hats when a funeral passed. All the same, people insured against funeral expenses with a penny-a-week policy, a £10 funeral grant was payable on Co-op passbooks, and people still feared finishing up "down the Union" through lack of funds at the end.

A LABOUR OF LOVE

The word social is bandied about endlessly these days as an adjective — social workers, social misfits, social climbers and social status. In the twenties and thirties social was a noun, and a compelling one. It meant an enjoyable get-together at which everyone contributed something to the enjoyment of all. The programme began with a slap-up high tea, then followed brief speeches, games, dancing, an impromptu concert, community singing, more dancing and "Auld Lang Syne" on the stroke of midnight.

Groups of people with similar interests would arrange socials to keep in touch during the winter. Hobby sharers, trade colleagues, church folk, political workers, sports fans, musicians, collectors, amateur artists and scientists and workers for the general weal gathered for these friendly evenings which were less formal and more enjoyable than dinners. Entertainment was home-made and audiences indulgent.

Dorothy, Margaret and Gertie Mandeville aged 13, eight and five attended the 1929 St John Ambulance social which was organised by their father as a labour of love to raise money for the motor ambulance fund. Between them Margaret and Gertie have remembered everything connected with the event and set it down. I remember socials too, and their story typifies those evenings half a century ago that brought us so much pleasure.

Mr William Mandeville, though only five feet one inch in height, was not St John Chief Cadet Officer for 35 years for nothing — he was an excellent organiser who foresaw every possible difficulty, and he began planning the social some months beforehand. The children did not share in this, as their bedtime was 6 pm, and when they had gone William began to sketch out the programme.

First, 80 tickets had to be prepared, and with no aids like word processors or photo-copiers available he approached Aunt Edith who could use one of those new-fangled typewriters and persuaded her to undertake the monotonous typing job. The tickets were priced at 1s 6d, which was about as much as most people could afford. Next he obtained the evening's rental charge for every suitable room before settling with a clear conscience on the one he favoured — the Co-op and Labour Institute in Newland Street (a slight conflict in one way, as he was a Conservative).

The Institute, demolished in the run-up to the Newlands development, had a narrow entrance between shops, and stairs led to a large room, a small room, kitchen, washroom and two lavatories. It was respectable enough to host such gatherings as the Art Exhibition, often opened by a national figure, though by today's standards its facilities were primitive. But there was one big advantage — it was central. Nearly everybody walked in those days, so that if the night of the social turned out wet nobody would have too far to go in the rain.

The venue settled, Mr Mandeville considered the programme. With lots of talent available in those days it was easy to engage a band for dancing — piano, violin and drums — and a group of entertainers, in this case Charlie Watts, Bob Roberts and Charlie Beeby from the Co-op Male Voice Choir. A much harder job was to think of plenty of games suitable for people of all ages. Bedtime was postponed while he called for help and advice from his young daughters. Had they played any new games at school? Or heard of any? Or thought of any? Or played any at friends' parties?

Says Gertie: "Most of those we suggested were too lively for older people coming to the social, and we used to get rather cross, convinced that we youngsters would not enjoy ourselves, though in fact we always did, and looked forward to the social for at least two months beforehand."

At the start of the evening it was important to get people talking to one another, so games chosen as ice-breakers were word puzzles. Guests might have the names of animals pinned on their backs and need to go round asking questions to find out what animal they were, or be faced with the challenge of extracting the names of counties, towns and rivers from mixed up letters, or be asked to fit names to photographs and extracts from press cuttings: "Dad gave all three of us jobs preparing these games. We had to produce little cards and notices in our best writing and find pins, drawing pins and string to attach them to people's backs or the walls. All the larger props for each game were tied together in readiness so that on the night nothing could be forgotten, and the smaller things went into our holiday case, a light brown cardboard object which had two clasps and no lock. Friends donated prizes for the games which we packaged nicely and put safely away in readiness."

Meanwhile Mrs Mandeville was busy making new party dresses for the girls. Like many Kettering mothers she was expert with her sewing machine, and had her own system: "We had new clothes twice a year — a dress specially for the social, and a complete new outfit to wear on Easter Sunday. Our dresses were made from hand-me-downs, but Mother prided herself that they were newly created from scratch. A dress for re-use would be unpicked, the material washed and pressed, and cut to a completely different pattern to make a fresh garment. Most of our friends had to endure lifted shoulders and hems, which I think is why many old photographs show 'the dropped waistline.' Our coats were cut out by Mr Fairgreave, a qualified tailor who worked in a converted wash house at the bottom of his garden. The coats and dresses were always wool or silk, and I find it very hard now to be satisfied with man-made fibres, which have only one thing in their favour — easy care.

"The style of our party dresses was always the same — short puffed sleeves, skirt gathered to the waist, buttons and frills to decorate, and the inevitable sash. The sash was a status symbol. A proud housewife would try to get a good wide sash for her daughters on these occasions from ribbons costing a penny a yard for half an inch in width up to sixpence a yard for three or four inches. People could tell by your sashes and hair ribbons how well looked after you were."

For the social, Margaret and Gertie wore wider than usual dark green sashes with their dresses of pale green silk, and silver shoes. It was snowing when the longed-for evening came, so when the sisters set off to walk to the Institute they were wearing old clothes, macs and wellington boots, and carried their new dresses carefully folded and packed into a small case. Gertie regarded the snowstorm with mixed feelings: "Mother was relieved to see it, as it would flatten my hair which a favourite aunt had put into curlers the previous night, asking if I wanted 'onions' or 'carrots.' Either way it resulted in an almighty frizz, which I loved but Mother hated. Dad walked with us from our house in Wellington Street. He told us to take our old school shoes with us. We wondered why, and found out when we arrived."

Mrs Mandeville had gone early, and at the hall, which Gertie remembered for its characteristic smell of damp wood, was busy with other wives who had volunteered to "do the food". This was an undertaking for specialists. Donations from the ambulance officers and their wives paid for the eatables, and much discussion had taken place to estimate quantities. How much bread and butter? Time needed to cut it by hand (much thinner than now)? How many sandwiches? How many each of potted meat or salmon and shrimp paste? How many gallons of tea? And — a vital decision — when to light the copper so that the water would boil at just the right moment?

"We now discovered why we had brought our old shoes. Dad told us to put them on, go into the big room and run and slide about as much as we liked. We couldn't believe our ears! We found the floor covered with white powder, and our job was to tear round until we had worked it in and made the floor slippery enough for dancing.

"This done, we were allowed to put on our new dresses and were then forbidden to run about. Once again we were expected to be on our best behaviour, and were told to sit down and sit still. We were glad of the rest, and giggled when we thought someone might slip on our well-polished floor, but when things warmed up it was usually one of us who fell and had to be taken to the small room to suffer the indignity of having splinters removed.

"Nearer teatime Mother came to check our dresses, and we had to take them off and remove our liberty bodices (a great treat) because the buttons were showing underneath the fine silk. Such was our modesty that we were glad we'd arrived first so that such things could be done in privacy. It was considered wise to go to the lavatory before the grown-ups needed it. There was only one cloakroom with two lavatories in it. They were not marked for ladies or gents, but everyone seemed to know which was which. If anyone wanted to change their clothes, the gentlemen in the room made discreet exits on request. The main body of guests were now arriving, some saying how pretty we looked. I felt like a princess, and acted accordingly!''

Too timid to go into the big room on her own, and waiting for Dorothy and Margaret, Gertie lifted the lid of a big box. To her horror a skeleton gazed up at her — one kept by St John for anatomy classes. Nearby was a wheeled stretcher, and in a cupboard an assortment of splints and bandages. The Institute was one of the town's ambulance stations as well as the venue for the social. Nothing like mixing pleasure with business.

When the girls returned to the big room they saw how much work had gone into the preparations: ''It was a sight for our young eyes. Trestle tables had been placed all over the room, covered by large white double damask tablecloths starched by each lady as if she had entered a competition, all hanging correctly in four screen folds at the corners. On each table was a pot of pretty flowers and plates, knives, forks and spoons all correctly laid, with place settings in Dad's copperplate. All items were lent by the families concerned, second best being specified so that there would not be too much grief if any were broken or lost. The cutlery bore a multitude of different coloured cottons round the handles so that the owners could easily reclaim their property.

''At intervals, so that everyone could reach them without losing their manners, were plates of ham, pork pie, tinned salmon, pickles, lettuce, tomatoes and thinly sliced cucumber in vinegar and pepper. There was celery for those brave enough to make a noise eating it, tinned fruit and the inevitable jellies.

''There were always jellies at parties and we loved them. I think they must have been made with real fruit in those days — they are certainly not so popular now. And of course there was plenty of bread and butter to eat with the tinned fruit. It was not polite to eat the fruit on its own, as this made you look as though you only wanted the good things of life.''

The sisters realised that they were very hungry, as their mother had deliberately given them no tea at home. This was so that they should not commit the sin of leaving anything on their plates. All plates had to be left clean and no food wasted. The guests were now sitting at the tables chatting happily. Everyone was eager to begin, and they awaited the principal visitors.

"Mr Dyson the corps superintendent came in with a big flourish accompanied by quiet and homely Mrs Dyson, and instantly the whole noise level seemed to be raised. He had such a large voice, projected through an equally large moustache, that it seemed to set the volume. There was another delay while guests played a word game, until with due ceremony well timed for a grand entrance in walked Dr Drake-Lee. He was always the guest of honour in acknowledgement of the way in which he encouraged St John's work and gave up time to judge our first aid competitions."

Such was the esteem in which the doctor was held that a hush fell over the gathering until Mr Mandeville as chairman welcomed him and asked him to say grace. This was the green light for which Dorothy, Margaret and Gertie had been waiting for so long: "With manners expected of us we tried to gorge ourselves without making it too obvious, and helped the food disappear except for one sandwich and one cake left on each plate. No-one was impolite enough to take the last one, for leaving it was a sign to your hosts that you had had sufficient. This was rather nice for us, as these 'polite cakes' were gathered up afterwards, and as Dad had the largest family they were given to him."

For the meal the girls did not sit with their parents. Showing great faith in their manners their father had split them up and placed them next to people who had come to the social alone: "Dad knew exactly what he was doing when he positioned us among the guests. There is nothing so good as a child beside them to start people talking." The sisters still have mental pictures of members of well-known families who were there — Woolmers, Cricks, Lentons, Browns, Sweetings, Thompsons, Millers, Fosters, Bill Line and Mr Dyson's son Noel — all people to whom neighbourhoods turned for help when accidents happened.

When the speeches came on the three girls sat staring at the few remaining cakes and applauding when the adults did. Then came their father's remarks which they had already heard a few times when he rehearsed them at home. They laughed at his "little witty bits", clapped, and were very proud to see the due respect accorded him by the company.

After the meal, tables were cleared and volunteers did the washing up, giving those who had prepared the repast a well-earned rest: "Each of the ladies provided two tea towels, preferably used ones, as new towels were so thick and well made that they were difficult to use until they had been washed several times. This meant of course that Mum spent the previous week getting her used ones whiter than white with a tablet of Sunlight soap and 'elbow grease'. There was a great deal of pride in such things. With washing-up finished, others claimed their crockery and cutlery back, and we helped with everything and made lots of new friends. The rest of the year we should have to be seen and not heard, but this was our day of acceptance by adults and we made the most of it."

Chairs were moved back and tables folded away to clear the floor for games, and Mr Mandeville announced the winner of the first one, held before tea. The prize for this was substantial, to get people to join in the other games, and he held the floor giving out instructions for playing a lively competition to cover the noise of the band unpacking and tuning up: "At this point we would play 'apples on strings' or encourage rival teams to pass a balloon round without using hands. One year we were very daring and tied up two whole lines of people by passing string through the sleeves of dresses and coats, then mixing up the competitors to see which team untangled themselves first, but this game caused so much confusion that Dad never repeated it."

Order of the programme when the band was ready to play was two dances followed by a game. This was a great moment for the young sisters, who were all accomplished little dancers: "Our parents could not afford 1s 6d a week each for attendance at a private school of dancing, but we went to the Co-op country dancing classes at only 2d a session, which were a sheer joy. The first dance at the social was a military two-step to 'Tipperary', and when we were all dancing merrily the music stopped and Dad ordered us to make it a progressive dance so that each gentleman moved to the next lady. Being so small I was rather embarrassed as I approached a very tall man, but thanks to my twopenny dancing classes my competence overcame the height problem and I received a pleasant smile before my partner progressed. Fortunately most men were around five feet six inches. They all made sure we children enjoyed dancing with them, and I am certain no other partners had spent so much time trying to make themselves beautiful as we had. We were all well groomed, fresh looking and well mannered, even if we did smell of Sunlight soap with a tinge of mothballs.''

They really had fun in the games, even getting to the point where most of the men, who had never tried before, accepted the challenge to walk about on stilts. With so many ambulance personnel on duty in case of a tumble it would have been sheer cowardice to refuse. Gertie adds: ''Looking back, I am puzzled by one thing — most of the children there were girls. Only two boys attended, and they spent most of their time watching the drummer. We were able to show off to our hearts' content, and I remember even breaking into a spontaneous dance when everybody else was resting, and getting applause.''

There were two periods for entertainment. The male trio started off the concert with 'Dandelion, Daisy and Daffodil', a slightly naughty song about three ladies and some long grass: ''The adults laughed their heads off, so we did too. Then the trio showed their real skill with 'Come into the garden, Maud' and 'The Merry Pipes of Pan'. Anyone who wished could now entertain, and we had volunteers alternating with such favourites as 'Albert and the Lion' and 'When I'm Cleaning Windows' besides 'Who is Sylvia?' and 'My Old Dutch'. It didn't matter who rendered songs or how they performed so long as people had a go. No-one pretended to be perfect, they just did their best, and very enjoyable it was.''

That year Mr and Mrs Mandeville thought the girls might sing a song. Dorothy played the piano moderately well, and was to accompany Margaret and Gertie: ''I forget what the song was, but we each had a line to sing on our own, one line together, and each in turn would lead the chorus. Dorothy played the introduction and sang her line, Margaret followed with hers, and next it was my turn, but I just clenched my hands, stood as if all I wanted was the toilet, and giggled helplessly. My sisters gallantly carried on, but the next time round the same thing happened. They bravely went on to the third verse, but still no words from me.

"This time everyone was doubled up with laughter at my lack of co-operation. I was totally ignoring digs in the ribs from Margaret's elbow, trying to get me started. My giggles were infectious, the audience were in tears, and I was duly hailed star of the evening, having done nothing!"

About 9.30 the room seemed to have more space in it, and games were more difficult to organise. The reason was that older folk had got tired, and men who wanted a quick drink had disappeared to the Fleur de Lys opposite. To offset this, the ladies were bringing round cups of tea and some of the remaining sandwiches.

But this quiet spell was only a breather. Soon Walter Dyson, a great favourite with the children, reappeared and continued blowing up a seemingly endless supply of balloons, which restarted the fun as they were punted about. Men returned from the "Flue", the band was refreshed, and the Mandeville magic got everybody back on the floor for a spot waltz and the best prize of the evening. Nobody was going to miss the chance of winning a nice tin of talcum powder and a bottle of bath cubes.

As the clock ticks on towards midnight, Gertie's account brings the evening to a close with a nice piece of observation: "Soon it seemed a good moment to ask the Male Voice Choir members to lead community singing. Each year the same songs from World War I were sung. They just sounded old to us, but each generation seems eventually to find pleasure in the songs their parents sang, and a few from World War II are being rearranged now. During the songs Dad was busy in a corner checking the details and preparing to wind up the evening, and we had just enough energy left to sing 'Should auld acquaintance . . . .' promptly at midnight when Sunday began, and it was all over for another year."

In the chilly cloakroom the family prepared for the walk home through hushed and snowy streets. Their coats, hanging on top of one another on one of the dozen pegs, still felt cold and wet, and most people seemed to be searching for one or other of their outdoor boots. Going along, they talked excitedly about the events of the evening. Back in the house, bedroom candles were lit, and it was up the wooden hill, down sheet lane, over the hills and back again. This was the only day in the year when the sisters could stay up so late, and they were actually allowed to fall into bed having only washed their hands. . . .

"Next morning Dad was up early, waking us gently with a cup of tea and cleaning our shoes for church. 'How do you think it went?' he asked, with a twinkle in his eye. He knew very well that his carefully rehearsed plans had not failed, and the social had been another success. Now his reward, and the only one he ever asked, was to hear us say 'It was lovely, wish it was tonight.' And so we began to discuss all the small happenings, trying to hang on to the pleasure of it as long as possible.

"Discos are the thing at the moment. It is not unusual at a very early age to be asked to bring a bottle to a party. Even with this extra seeming stimulation, when I have asked my children if they enjoyed their party the usual answer is 'Not all that much.' Perhaps we have failed them in some way by being too busy to continue with organising socials, or perhaps their senses are too dulled to appreciate enjoyment? I am sure Dad was right — leave the drink outside. Those who want it will go and get it, and the rest can enjoy themselves. If he was here to organise a social, I am absolutely certain everyone would enjoy it, even now."

Gertie adds that since she wrote her story of the 1929 social the family has revived the idea, organised several present-day socials, and enjoyed old-time fun.

THEATRES AND CINEMAS

Kettering's love affair with the theatre began in mid-Victorian days with Tom Payne who ran Payne's Penny Gaff. It was said that his family were wandering players who liked the town and stayed. The gaff was a portable theatre which he stored in sections on a patch of ground in Field Street and erected at one of the inn yards when a travelling company wanted to put on a show. The players stayed at or near the inn, performed for little more than beer, bread and board, and attracted patrons for the brewers. The gaff was primitive — walls and roof of wood and canvas, planks across barrels for seats, and alfresco toilet arrangements.

Next, Tom erected a permanent theatre on the west side of Field Street. Admission was 1½d, increased to 2d for seats by the coke stove in winter, and in summer the rear of the stage was thrown open to increase ventilation and provide a backcloth of open country looking across to the railway, as Bayes and Carlton Streets were not then built. One production was a railway thriller, and the plot turned on the passage of a real express which the audience could see and hear through the open stage. One night the train was late, the actors were left gagging to kill time, and the audience got the giggles as crime turned to comedy. Plays included blood-curdlers like *Murder in the Red Barn* and *The Demon Barber of Fleet Street*, but the Bard of Avon held his own with frequent visits by enthusiastic companies so that Shakespeare Cottages became the official address of the row next to the theatre.

Payne faced competition from Wild's gaff in Newland Street and from shows brought to the fair by Taylors and Thurstons. He sometimes ran short of cash, and when the gas company's bill was overdue they sent a collector who arrived during the

75

show and threatened to turn off the lighting. Payne was acting in the play, but was unabashed when a scene shifter rushed on to the stage with "Master, the gas man's come." In Roman costume, he brandished his sword and declaimed "Away, slave. Tell him I'll meet him at Stanion."

The gaffs died out when the Victoria Hall, a large and completely equipped theatre and public hall opened in Gold Street in 1888. It was built by a local company whose directors included Dr J. W. Dryland, solicitor C. W. Stringer, brewer John Elworthy, builder H. Henson, shoe manufacturer W. C. East, and landed proprietor H. Sartoris of Rushden Hall, strengthened by members with theatre experience elsewhere and Captain Gray as secretary. There were seats for 900 in stalls, balcony and gallery, and the stall seats could be removed to clear the hall for dinners, dances and other events. Theatre prices catered for everyone — stalls 2d, 3d, 6d, 9d and 1s, balcony 6d and gallery 4d.

Kettering Public Hall Co. ran the Vic successfully for 20 years with a succession of plays, musicals and variety shows, sandwiching in local productions and all the major social events, but by 1907 the responsibility was growing too heavy for the founders. The hall passed to Alf Bailey & Co., whose business manager Bert Bailey was keen to promote the theatre, and under him many spectacular touring shows were staged up to and through the first world war. By 1920 big changes were in the air. Hollywood was established, silent films were being made in great numbers, and the Vic management realised that a theatre which was not also a cinema could not survive.

They embarked on a major reconstruction and reopened as the Victoria Picture House, still run by a local syndicate but no longer a public hall. Builders had removed the gallery and reconstructed the balcony with a sloping floor, tip-up seats could seat 850 patrons in complete comfort, and a new Victoria Restaurant had been added offering a full service of meals from 11 am to 9.30 pm. The big stage was retained for use when required, and the operating box was beyond it, allowing for films to be projected from behind the screen. The Gold Street frontage was remodelled to provide a wide entrance sheltered by a glass canopy. Prices were 6d, 9d and 1s for stalls and 1s 6d balcony and Mary Pickford in *The Ragamuffin* was the opener.

The silent film years were a great era for the Vic, which prided itself on being the best cinema in town. A solo pianist to accompany the films was not enough — from the start music was a feature, with intervals for popular melodies played by instrumentalists under Mrs Melbourne, styled the directress. Roy Goodfellow remembers that by 1926 the theatre orchestra was led by Maurice Friedman, who was brought in specially and composed a descriptive piece entitled 'The Bells of Kettering'. Elsie, Roy's mother, was pianist and violinist, Ada Calvert played saxophone and clarinet, and a lady named Biddy the drums. Eventually towards the end of the silent film days the orchestra grew to a ten-piece combination presenting miniature concerts in the intervals. The leader was John Sugden who as a young man had attended the Brussels Music Conservatoire specialising in the violin, played with the Halle Orchestra, and indulged his love of cricket by turning out with Yorkshire 2nd XI. It was the end of a way of life in 1929 when silent films clicked away into history and suddenly talkies ruled the world of the cinema.

The anticipated flood of patrons when at last good quality sound films were produced in quantity led to the purchase of the Vic by the expanding Odeon chain. Kettering builders O. P. Drever demolished the familiar interior which had served for over 40 years and remodelled it as a luxury cinema, installing a new projector room behind the balcony and increasing the seating to 1,090, 740 in the stalls and 350 in the balcony. Mr Stephen Schilizzi of Loddington Hall declared the building open on September 19, 1936, with Eddie Cantor in Strike Me Pink as the attraction.

A new era of prosperity for the Vic extended for 24 years through the second world war and up to 1950 when, on October 29, Rank Leisure Services closed it with Norman Wisdom in There Was A Crooked Man as the finale. Bingo was not successful, and after standing for a melancholy time with its entrance bricked up, the sound old building which had served the town uncommonly well was demolished in 1974. The site is occupied by shops on the western side of the Newlands Centre.

The Vic's main rival started life as the Avenue Theatre, Russell Street, opened in 1903 by Frank Payne who had commissioned his brother William to build it. They were sons of Tom Payne who had owned Payne's Penny Gaff. A fantastic week of music launched the Avenue. The Grand English Opera Company opened with *Faust* and gave a change of programme every evening with *Maritana*, *The Lily of Killarney*, *Tannhauser*, *Il Trovatore* and *Daughter of the Regiment*. Seating was 800, prices 2d, 4d, 6d and 9d stalls, and 6d and 9d balcony.

Though away from the town centre the Avenue had all the essentials for success. It stood amid residential streets which housed potential patrons, offered digs for performers, and provided unlimited waiting space for horse transport bringing country folk to the shows. The landladies were good friends to the stage people, and at least once gave practical help when a manager decamped with the takings, leaving his company stranded. They contributed more than enough to send their guests on to the next town.

Another attraction was the Avenue Hotel, at just the right distance from the theatre for patrons to go for a stroll and a drink at the interval, often getting the added pleasure of meeting performers who had slipped out for a refresher. The Avenue has kept its name, and is a reminder of the colourful days of the Edwardian live theatre.

Roller skating had a vogue in 1908, and the Avenue Theatre was converted to a rink, but this was a mistake and in 1910 it reopened as the Coliseum, modestly adopting the name of the 50,000-seat amphitheatre in ancient Rome. A sign of changing times was the provision of a projector for films if needed between stage acts. The Col, as it was affectionately called, passed through the hands of a number of lessees including builder O. P. Drever before in 1932 Jack Sherwood became managing director and then owner. He made great improvements, equipped the theatre for talkies, and renamed it the New Coliseum.

Jack, from Tipton, Staffordshire, was son-in-law of Frank Payne, the original owner, and renewal of the family connection was warmly welcomed. David Bradshaw remembers him as a tall, willowy man-about-town, always elegant and impeccably dressed and seldom arriving in his streamlined saloon without his wife May who was renowned for her London fashions. Jack was softly-spoken and agreeable, and proud of his theatre and its star-studded history. Such top-liners as Gladys Cooper, Harry Tate, Buffalo Bill, Gracie Fields, Charlie Chaplin and Lily Langtry had graced its boards.

A new chapter was written on April 6, 1936. In a few hours in the middle of the night the Coliseum was destroyed by fire. Bob Stephenson, a reporter on the *Evening Telegraph*, was lodging in York Road with Mrs Morris of Bible Class and football team fame. His room overlooked Russell Street, and along with the whole neighbourhood he was awakened by a tremendous crash when the roof caved in. As firemen fought to contain the flames he wrote a minute-by-minute account from his vantage point. They could not save the building, but they rescued 12,000 feet of film (*The Singing Vagabond* starring Gene Autrey and *Three Wise Guys* starring Robert Young and Betty Furness along with Paramount News) which would have exploded if the fire had reached the operating box first, and the theatre cat saved herself. Dodging the flames and hundreds of gallons of water she emerged from the basement unhurt.

David Bradshaw had an even closer view than Bob Stephenson. He was a little boy at the time, living just opposite the theatre's main entrance: "I remember my mother shaking me as I woke from a deep sleep. 'Get up quickly,' Mother said, 'the Coliseum is on fire.' She cradled me in her arms, swept out of the bedroom which was already hot from the flames, and ran with me to the kitchen. I could feel her trembling, and heard my father rousing my grandmother and sister. There was a terrifying splashing as the firemen hosed our house to cool the blistering woodwork and walls.

"In the back gardens we found neighbours huddled in overcoats over their night clothes, trying to console one another. They carried pets and cherished possessions, and the little girls had rescued their dolls. Daylight revealed nothing left of the Coliseum but smouldering ashes and the high outer wall which by remaining standing had contained the worst of the heat and saved our houses. All trace of the fine old theatre vanished when with long poles and a concerted heave the firemen toppled the wall, leaving only broken bricks and dust."

David heard that the fire was discovered by Harold Ball, the railway driver next door, who saw flames already flickering from the top of the building when he came home in the early hours. So great was the heat that when claims were assessed all the houses in the vicinity of the fire were reglazed and repainted at the expense of the insurers. It must have been a fearful and exciting night. Among mementoes were tip-up seats pulled clear by Frank Evans the Mill Road barber and installed for customers in his shop.

From the ashes rose a vastly improved super cinema and theatre called the Savoy, opened on May 21, 1938 by Councillor Walter Dyson in person and Spencer Tracey on film in *Big City*. Seating was for 1,131 — 774 in the stalls and 357 in the circle. The new proscenium was 42 feet wide, almost double the old one, and admission was 9d, 1s, 1s 6d and 2s 6d stalls, balcony 1s 6d and 2s 6d.

David found the rebuilding a source of endless interest and do-it-yourself materials from thrown-away oddments: "O. P. Drever cleared the site, and the main contractor was Leyton of London. For years afterwards our shoes were repaired by my father with rubber pieces cast aside by the workmen when they laid the foyer floor. When it was opened notable guests wore black ties and evening dresses, and the giant neon sign SAVOY lit the whole street. My grandmother never used her own light again until the wartime blackout, but sat every evening with her curtains drawn back, basking in the neon glow and studying the arrivals and departures at the dome of delight across the road."

Troise and his Mandoliers played to packed audiences for the opening week, Owen Naires followed with his colossal West End success *The Belle of New York*, then came Harry K. Barnes who had won screen fame for his role as *The Scarlet Pimpernel*, Tommy Trinder who played football with the children in the street, Duggie Wakefield, Sandy Powell, Will Fyfe, Ted Ray in *Black Velvet*, George Robey and many others.

"When war was declared in 1939 our lovely neon lights went out, but the shows continued apart from a short break in 1940 when Princess Patricia's Canadian Light Infantry arrived with their camouflaged transport and were billeted in the theatre before going on to Wicksteed Park and land off Linden Avenue. Many great stars performed in the provinces, and Kettering which provided homes for thousands of young evacuees was a prime destination. Ella Shields sang 'Burlington Bertie' at the Savoy, and even when the main attraction of the week was a major film, cine-variety was introduced with four-star acts between showings. Two of the great radio shows of the 1940s, *Happidrome* and *Itma*, came live to the Savoy, though Tommy

Handley had died by then. Dickie 'Stinker' Murdoch of *Band Waggon* drew huge crowds, and Lord John Sanger brought his circus. Three enormous elephants came down Russell Street every night from the Angel Hotel stables where they were billeted, everyone turning out to watch and gardeners at the ready with shovels and buckets.''

In 1944 Clifton Cinemas took over, presenting stage shows by top artists and name bands until 1953, and a popular innovation was a lease for plays to Northampton Repertory Company. Star Cinemas acquired control in 1961, and from 1968 the stalls were reserved for bingo while the balcony became two small cinemas, Studios 1 and 2. Savoy Buildings now house the Stardust Bingo Club and the town's surviving cinema, the Ohio.

Kettering's third theatre and cinema was in Market Place, by turns Vint's Electric Palace, the Palace, and the Hippodrome. The building, now shops, is of great interest as it was the Town Hall and Corn Exchange, erected in 1854 to the design of Edmund Law of Northampton, also architect for the Old Grammar School in Gold Street, demolished in 1964. When no longer needed as offices and corn market it served for a time as the public library under Miss Kate Pierce, then in 1909 it became vacant and caught the interest of Leon Vint, owner of a cinema chain. He saw an opening in Kettering as the Avenue Theatre had switched to roller skating, and opened his new venture as Vint's Electric Palace, fully equipped for stage shows and moving pictures. Admission was 2d, 3d and 6d stalls, balcony 9d, and there were two houses at 7 pm and 9 pm. Vint did not stay when the Avenue reopened as the Coliseum, and sold out to John Covington, a prosperous Kettering coal merchant and businessman who shortened the name to the Palace. Among stars who came were Harry Tate, Lily Langtry, G. H. Elliott the Chocolate Coloured Coon, and Dr Bodie the electrical wizard who drew a crowd looping round the Market Place. Many years before talkies the Palace tried to provide dialogue for silent pictures by placing an actor and actress behind the screen reading from a script, but the idea was soon dropped.

After five years Covington sold to Fred Hawkins who re-titled the theatre the Hippodrome, a throwback to Greek equestrian amphitheatres rivalling the Coliseum in evoking magnificence, but he dropped the stage acts in favour of continuous film shows from 6.15 pm to 10.30 pm, so ending an eventful ten years in which Kettering people had three live theatres. Hawkins went bankrupt in 1922, and it was goodbye to the Hippodrome, its loss leaving a decided gap as it had been the liveliest of the cinemas, favoured by a youthful and high-spirited audience. John Andrew as a boy used to get in on Saturday afternoons for a penny downstairs — "sit where you like" — and if he had a halfpenny to buy an ounce of fig toffee he felt rich. The programme would consist of a big picture, say Pearl White in *The Big Secret*, supported by an instalment of a 10- or 12-episode serial, maybe *The Great Archer*, with a newsreel and comedy. Advertisement slides were shown, among them one for Charnleys the opticians.

Jack Tingle went there as a boy when younger patrons were skylarking and subjecting the long-suffering pianist who accompanied the films to a barrage of apple cores, orange peel and peanut shells. If attempts were made to eject them, Jack and his mates used to climb the cast iron pillars supporting the roof, using the mouldings as footholds, and above balcony height they could sit in metal circles which were part of the design and continue the bombardment in safety.

The pianist, whom John Andrew described as an Austrian with a repertoire of old tunes like 'I'm For Ever Blowing Bubbles' pressed on regardless, but eventually he and his piano were enclosed in a protective cage of chicken wire, which spoilt the fun. Today the building stands virtually intact and deserves to be treated as the striking landmark it is. The words COMEDY DRAMA OPERA in gold lettering have still not vanished from the stonework.

Demise of the Hippodrome left the Vic, the Coliseum and two new cinemas, the Pavilion and the Empire to share the market. The Pavilion, at the northern end of High Street where Superdrug stands was built by the Rotherham Electric Theatre Co. in 1913 on the site of John Northern's house. With prices at first 2d, 4d, 6d and 9d it was comfortable, but had an air of being built down to a price. Two aisles descending a sloping floor gave access to 650 seats, and the place was really a huge brick barn with the steel roof supports remaining visible.

For many years there was no foyer, and to reduce the draught heavy velvet curtains hung inside the doors on wooden rings on a pole, making a loud clacking as usherettes whipped them to and fro. There was standing room for late-comers who could lean on a rail behind the rear stalls until seats became vacant. What it lacked in interior appointments the Pavilion atoned for with its entrance. Patrons climbed six marble steps to the paybox, and 48 coloured lamps justified the original title of the County Electric Pavilion. Silent films demanded musical accompaniment, and Tom Hart remembers that his mother, May Martin, had a sister Florence who used to double up by playing the piano at the Pavilion on weekdays and the organ at Toller Church across the road on Sundays. The girls were two of the eight daughters of Charles Martin, tailor, of Wellington Street.

Ted Grove saw one of the first primitive attempts to present talking pictures at the Pavilion. There was no soundtrack on the film, but someone near the screen had the job of synchronising a disc recording with the picture, which left a lot to be desired. The Pavilion commissionaire tried to freshen the air, patrolling the aisles with a big flit spray loaded with disinfectant, and Philip Hague remembers that another of his duties was to walk round with a pole and prod any of the younger element who were misbehaving.

In 1927 the Pavilion passed from Mutton & Shapiro of Nottingham to Gaumont-British who renamed it the Gaumont Pavilion and introduced soundtrack talkies in 1929. There was a long run until 1953 when Joan Collins in person and *Genevieve*

Kettering cinema pioneer Harry Bamford had practical experience. A professional photographer, he gave village lantern shows, then exhibited his own films, and with partners built the Empire after the 1914-18 war. He visualised a super cinema on the Eskdaill Street-Stamford Road corner. (Joan Payne)

reopened it after redecoration and the addition of a much-needed foyer, but faced with the growth of TV, Rank Leisure Services closed it in 1959 with *Last Train From Gun Hill*. In 1960, after 47 years, the Pav fell before the bulldozers.

In 1921 a newcomer to the entertainment world was the Empire in Eskdaill Street, opened by partners T. H. Bamford, A. Cheaney and H. G. Roughton. It grew from a threepenny gaff which Mr Bamford took round the villages by pony and trap, accompanied by a member of Alf Bailey's family who played a violin and led community singing. The gaff showed slides to which Mr Bamford gave a commentary, and as he had a photographer's business in Montagu Street many of them were topical. Joan Payne, his step-daughter remembers that when she was little the Empire booked *The Thundering Herd* (Jack Holt, Lois Wilson and Noah Beery) and White Elk, an Indian chief, came with it. He did a war dance on the roof of the shop at the Eskdaill Street corner which always drew crowds, and described the film in broken English. He was chief of a tribe which took part in making the film.

At first admission was 5d, 9d, 1s and 1s 6d for the stalls, with the balcony 1s 3d, but this was too costly for the times and the stalls were reduced to 3d, 5d, 9d and 1s. The 400 seats included a number of doubles in the balcony, intended for young lovers and dubbed "hugging hutches". These gained the Empire publicity, but they had disadvantages. Ted Grove found them singularly uncomfortable when shared with a complete stranger of the same sex, and Jack Tingle discovered that spots of water fell from the ceiling and splashed down the back of his neck. He reported that the roof leaked, but investigation showed that with a full house in cold weather the moisture from patrons' breath condensed on the ceiling and descended in droplets.

Ted's outstanding Empire memory is of cliff-hanging serials in 15-minute episodes. They always ended when excitement was at its height, the milk train six feet from the heroine bound to the rails, only to fade into "Don't miss next week's exciting instalment." I always suspected the producer of cheating when it turned out the following week that the heroine had already undone a vital knot and was able to roll clear, but it was all part of the game and kept the box office busy.

Jack Sherwood acquired the Empire, and closed it on June 19,

1954. Today it is the Selecta car spares centre with big windows lighting the once-dark auditorium. A relic of past glories is the filled-in entrance arch, still distinguished by its ornamentation.

Last to appear was the Regal, a purpose-built super-cinema which cost £10,000 to build in 1936 (multiply by 100 for today's equivalent price) and was opened by Earl Spencer. I attended the event, and am pretty sure I had to wear a dinner jacket, but the only thing I remember clearly is that one of the films was three-dimensional, and to view it we had to put on cardboard specs with one eyepiece red and the other green. Without them the film was visual gibberish, but wearing them made moving objects like advancing trains seem to leap out into the audience. The main film was *Everything is Rhythm* starring Harry Roy and his band, and on stage were Petulengro and his Ladies Hussar Band of piano accordionists.

The Regal, later the Granada and now a bingo and social club, had an impressive foyer, a large stage which enabled it to be used as a concert venue, and a good restaurant. Seating was 1,742, 1,200 in the stalls and the rest in the balcony. Ted Grove says: "It was very grand, and an attraction was the stage acts. I remember seeing Tommy Handley and his *Disorderly Room*, and I think I saw the young Morecambe and Wise there. Sunday celebrity concerts brought the big bands of the day." Sunday stage stars included Vera Lynn, Flanagan and Allen and many more famous people, with Geraldo, Joe Loss, Jack Hylton and Henry Hall among the bands and Reginald Foort with his immense transportable organ. Live show admission charges were 6d, 1s, 1s 6d, 2s, 2s 6d and 3s 6d. Film shows were much cheaper at 6d to 2s.

The manager was L. Morley-Clarke, who showed a rather less than tactful touch when he advertised for waitresses, usherettes and cashiers. Out of 300 applicants he accepted only one, a 15-years-old blonde, as showing the smiling prettiness and grace he required. He wanted two dozen, and talked of importing girls from Sevenoaks where the group had another cinema. Nowadays local patriots would show their reaction against such an insult, but in 1936 we just regarded it as a sign of LM-C's poor judgement and continued to stump up our shillings and sixpences.

The 1930s cinema and theatre chiefs held key positions in the town, and were personalities. I cannot remember a Pavilion manager, but Morley-Clarke was a big, buoyant individual who walked along under a broad-rimmed hat, somehow reflecting a little of Hollywood's glamour. Jack Sherwood was likeable, modest and rather diffident, while Mr Needham at the Vic was small and uncommunicative, his mind obviously on the day's problems as he hurried along High Street. Bert Dawson the Empire manager was alert and businesslike, usually visibly on duty supervising the start of proceedings each evening.

The Empire did not seem to need a commissionaire, and I never remember queueing there, but the other cinemas had Ruritanean officers in peaked caps and gold braid whose job was to marshal the patrons into orderly queues. Mr Turner the Pavilion commissionaire, lived next to Jim Dodge who remembers him as an ex-sergeant major: "You never got past him for an A Certificate film. When the old Vic was tiled in black and yellow he moved there and considered it promotion, as we all did. The nature of his employment meant that he was free in the mornings so that he became a distinguished gardener, specialising in chrysanthemums and possessing the only greenhouse at our end of the estate." Harry Ball, his opposite number at the Coliseum, had a parrot beloved of the children.

Patrons queued uncomplainingly in all but the worst weather. Continuous performances meant that the whole programme was shown three times, beginning in early afternoon and finishing about 10.30 pm. The first showing provided a pleasant excursion for people with leisure who could be home in time for tea, and they were succeeded in the evening by members of families who attended first house if they started work around 7.30 am next day and second house if they were nine-to-fivers. In between were patrons who were not particular about savouring a film from beginning to end, and could cope with the plot by seeing the conclusion first. They would go in at any time, departing when the point at which they had entered came round again.

The queues formed during the first evening performance in readiness for the second house, and as they waited the patrons who had gone in during the earlier showing and had their fill came out a few at a time. It fell to the usherettes to discover empty seats with their torches and inform the commissionaire, who would emerge shouting "Two ninepennies together", or "Two shillings in different parts", or maybe information about coveted back-row seats. Those who wished could then step forward and leave the queue, possibly paying more than they intended to get out of the wind and rain.

Inside the cinema they would find themselves in darkness until the usherette beckoned by waving her torch and guided them to the vacant seats, shining the beam along the row. All the patrons between the aisle and the empty places would have to stand up, raising their tip-up seats, leaning back by supporting themselves on the arms and pulling their feet away from being trodden on. The latecomers would insinuate themselves between these bulging figures, often overcoated or mackintoshed, and the backs of the seats in front, edging sideways amid grumbles about obscuring the screen until they were able to flop down in the empty seats. A danger was that they would miscalculate a sit heavily on the lap of some comatose sweet-sucking lady patron, eliciting a muffled scream or snarl of protest.

There was practical freemasonry among the people in each row. When the usherettes came round with sweets, cigarettes and ice creams on illuminated trays supported by straps around their necks, people would hand along loose coins with requests for ten Players, two tubs or a couple of chocolate bars. The money always arrived in the hands of the sales girl, who counted it in under her subdued tray lighting and sent back equal value in merchandise and change, which also returned safely.

Chocolates belonging to wealthier patrons were not always consumed, and I found as a youngster that when the lights came up after the last performance it paid to look under the seats on the way out, as occasionally some sated Croesus would have discarded a half-full box rather than cart it home.

Smoking was not then regarded as a health hazard, and the light from projection box to screen had to cut wandering wedges through a fog of cigarette smoke, which meant that there was a minor fire risk. People with both eyes on the screen, fumbling in darkness for ashtrays fixed to the seats were liable to miscalculate, spraying fag-end sparks around, and morning light would reveal scorched holes in overcoats. Science had not mastered another menace — fleas — and you might return home with a tiny companion busily inflicting itchy and lumpy bites. Fleas were picked up anywhere, in churches as well as cinemas, but regardless of origin they all had a fatal character defect —

greed. After gorging themselves on minute amounts of blood they became swollen and torpid, easily detectable under a strong light, and squashable between thumb nails. Mothers of young children were experts at flea-hunting.

Cinema publicity was well organised. Shops exhibited posters in exchange for free seats, and some gave cinema coupons to customers as change. The coupons, worth ½d each, had to be sent to Van Gessel & Co. who would exchange stated quantities for vouchers to be spent at the cinemas. All cinemas advertised in the *Evening Telegraph* and on Monday nights issued press seats so that a reporter could see the show and write the regulation three-inch review, but this privilege was not extended to the second half of the week and those films had to be described from handouts. The film companies issued endless photographs of stars and stories about them, good space-fillers if news was short, as the public appetite for information about film idols was never satisfied.

Unless a special attraction stayed for six days, each cinema by changing its programme halfway through the week showed two major films, two supporting films, several newsreels, and various short features, so that with five cinemas there was great variety with up to twenty different films on offer each seven days. Besides providing so much cheap entertainment an additional advantage of the cinema was that anyone with time to kill could find a warm and restful refuge at very moderate cost — something that has never been replaced.

Recapturing the atmosphere of the old cinemas I came across an article by Arthur Marshall, sparked off by the death of Mary Pickford. He recalled noises inseparable from the showing of silent films: "There was the rattle of brass curtain rings as the lady pianist deftly inserted herself into the orchestra pit, the click as she switched on that exciting beam of light to sort her music, the clatter and bang as the cheaper seats filled up, the hiss of the hygienic spray squirted over us by the haughty usherette, the hum of the electric motor that drew the silken curtains apart, and finally the moment when the pianist let fly with some exciting number ('Entry of the Gladiators', like as not) and the News flashed on."

Arthur remembered the clickety-click from the projection box, gasps of horror as Pearl White got herself into another disastrous pickle, and cheers from the youthful front rows as the sheriff's posse caught up with the robbers, followed by the swish of black sateen as the ice cream and lemonade vendeuse arrived. Other memories were the fusty absence of air that met you as you entered the cinema, and the gyrations of the poorly-positioned pianist anxiously craning her neck to keep up with the film and provide suitable music: "It would never do, while Lilian Gish as an unmarried mother was being turned out into the snow clutching a wee bundle, to come up with something jolly — unmarried mothers required minor keys and a good deal of rumbling with the left hand."

He found modern films sadly unenterprising by comparison with the treats of yesteryear when heroines were tied to railway lines, giant eagles swooped and made off with the baby, and ruined gamblers took the coward's way out: "Pola Negri vamped, Chaplin waddled his way into the sunset, Fairbanks senior flashed a sword, Valentino gave us his profile, and Mary Pickford with her riot of golden curls charmed everybody. Many of us miss them all yet. . . ."

Arthur forgot one of the irritating sounds. Always, as the final embrace or walk into the sunset approached, someone would sense that the film was about to end. A bang ruined the wistful moments as he (it was always he) leaped to his feet, released his tip-up seat and scooted for the door, hoping to get out before the National Anthem. Immediately there would be a shattering barrage as scores of others followed his example. Then, when the lights came up and a few bars of "The King" were played, the aisles would be full of struggling people trying to get to the doors. It was an unedifying spectacle, calculated to persuade Hitler that the English were not patriotic. I could never understand what all the hurry was about — but then, I did not have to answer a works hooter at 7.30 next morning.

How can we sum up the five cinemas that served Kettering so well before we obtained our private screens, sitting at home with our pictures, saved the trouble of going out, but deprived of the social contact and little adventures that made cinema-going such a splendid entertainment?

The picture houses have been called dream palaces, refuges for escapism, places where people could feel important because commissionaires and usherettes were in a sense their servants.

Nothing of the sort. The cinemas were pure and simple places of entertainment, opening as a matter of course every day including Bank Holidays, Christmas Day, Boxing Day and eventually Sundays, where hardworking people could get two or three hours of guaranteed peace and be told a story at the same time, accompanied by tuneful and satisfying music.

Patrons knew the managers, the operators, the usherettes and the splendid commissionaires by name, and liked special seats and favourite delicacies from the vending trays. In the films there was no nasty violence, no tedious jumping in and out of bed, and no bad language. It was family entertainment, and audiences apart from juvenile skylarking behaved impeccably.

As the cinema developed, children were specially considered. Clubs met on Saturday mornings to be shown junior films and receive pep talks instructing them in civilised conduct. Jim Dodge has memories: "Mum and Dad occasionally took us to the Coliseum before it burned down, and we became familiar with Will Hay, Moore Marriott and Graham Moffatt. We sat in

Junior fans greet a Charlie Chaplin lookalike who came in the 1920s to publicise one of Chaplin's films, The Pilgrim, at the Pavilion. With him is chief projectionist J. Stokes (trilby) and assistant Archie Mason.
(Fred Moore)

the balcony because the stalls were the province of un-
accompanied youngsters who booed and contrived to make
shadows on the screen. Central Avenue kids used to send one
of their number to buy a ticket so that when the lights went out
and the film started he could 'Push bar to open' and let his mates
in through the emergency exit. If the usherette called the
commissionaire in time they'd be led out jeering. If she didn't
they ducked along the rows and were safe, at least until the
interval.

"Older cousins took us to the Saturday morning children's
matinees at the Pavilion and Odeon where tickets were 3d. When
the Regal opened, round-towered and neon-lit, it undercut the
others by a penny, but merely dented their pre-eminence. At the
Pavilion we queued in a side alley and were fetched in batches
by the commissionaire, to whom the duty was clearly far from
a pleasure. The main attraction at the Pavilion was the weekly
Flash Gordon serial, apart from which its programme did not
differ significantly from the Odeon's.

"The usual pattern was three or four short films — Laurel and
Hardy perhaps, or the Three Stooges, a cartoon and a serial —
followed by an interval for the sale of ice cream. The second half
would be longer, often a cowboy film, perhaps Tom Mix or Buck
Rogers, covered in buckskin fringes and wearing a curvilinear
white stetson. Gene Autrey the singing cowboy we considered
cissy — we booed his songs and whistled when he kissed the
heroine at the end.

"The Odeon's Mickey Mouse Club was much more slickly
organised. We had to apply for membership before we were
given our badges, and there were singing sessions conducted
by the manager:

> Every Saturday morning, where do we go?
> Getting up to mischief? Oh dear, no!
> To the Mickey Mouse Club, with our badges on,
> Every Saturday morning at the ODEON!''

Everyone could find role models in their favourite stars whose
names by their very mention evoke a world of memories. In silent
days Mary Pickford, Clara Bow, Tom Mix, Wallace Beery,
Rudolph Valentino, Gloria Swanson, Charles Chaplin, Jackie
Coogan, Lon Chaney, George Arliss, Douglas Fairbanks, Pola

Negri, Will Rogers, Adolphe Menjou, Norma Shearer, Greta Garbo, Victor McLaglan, Dolores del Rio, Ronald Colman, Emil Jannings . . . everyone has his or her own list.

After talkies came, some silent stars dropped out, others found fresh fame and were joined by newcomers, the vast list including Lionel Barrymore, Marie Dressler, Helen Hayes, Frederick March, Charles Laughton, Claudette Colbert, Clark Gable, Bette Davis, Luise Rayner, Paul Muni, Merle Oberon, Wendy Hiller, and on, and on.

What a wonderful era the cinema brought us, concentrating literature, geography, history and science on to those silver screens. Today TV has the virtues of home-based entertainment, but lacks the human contact and glamour of even the smallest cinema. Moderns will say I don't know what I am talking about, but they never met their best girl on the corner, treated her to the best seat they could afford, shared a bag of sweets under the spell of a first-class film, and walked home under a silvery moon (or drizzle, it mattered not).

As I end this memory-trip, the BBC has just announced: "People are rediscovering the cinema-going habit." Somehow, I don't think it will be quite the same. The old films always sent us home feeling happy.

THE GENERAL HOSPITAL

When the plague raged in London in 1664-5, half the population fled and brought the infection to other places. Kettering was not immune. Between May 1665 and July 1666 the pestilence killed 78 people. They were buried outside the town, away from the prevailing wind, and graves found when Havelock Street was built two centuries later were believed to be theirs. In 1839 smallpox broke out. William James described it as a calamitous affliction, carrying off many people especially the young, and disfiguring victims it failed to kill.

Besides these two recorded epidemics there would have been many lesser outbreaks of infectious diseases which in those days could be killers on a large scale. If we add to them the other illnesses and injuries to which flesh is heir, with the hazards of primitive childbirth and the handicaps of old age, it becomes obvious that our forebears in their tiny cottages endured unimaginable miseries from which medical science mercifully shields us today.

Organised medical care was made available for the first time in 1801 by the establishment of the Kettering Dispensary, which despite its title was a small hospital with sufficient resources to treat about 300 patients every year. The surrounding gentry and leading town families funded it, and regularly cropping up in the minute book as subscribers are the Duke of Buccleuch, Lord Cardigan, Capt. Tibbits, the families of Maunsell, Toller, Gotch, Dolben, Lamb, Garrard, de Capell Brooke, Wallis, Wetherall and Paul, and various Kettering rectors.

Unmistakably the dispensary was a charity, and doubtless the patients knew it, for they were described as "the industrious poor who are willing to do without pecuniary assistance from their parishes, but must be driven to it if they do not obtain

93

medical aid free of expense." This definition came from Dr Skrimshire, who also wrote that he had "perceived in the objects relieved a proper gratitude, and a due sense of the benefits received." Dr Skrimshire sounds a hard man, and it seems that he, like Dr Bousfield and Dr Gibbon who also attended the poor, was an assistant employed by the Roughton family of doctors who for many years generously provided free treatment for the dispensary patients. Their practical goodwill went further, for the dispensary was part of the old workhouse in Workhouse Lane (Dryland Street) and lost its rooms when the new workhouse was opened in London Road in 1838. Dr William Roughton then provided new premises in a house he owned opposite his own residence in George Street, and his son Dr J. J. Roughton opened an accident hospital there, taking a constant interest in the work as medical officer for 40 years.

Records of the dispensary covering almost a century have survived thanks to Stanley Harris of Silvers the Market Place chemists. He discovered them in a room above the shop and gave them to the Public Library. They show that for many years the secretary was the Rev. James Hogg, otherwise known as the eccentric headmaster of Kettering Grammar School, whose annual reports display the utmost economy in words. Usually only two or three subscribers attended the annual meeting, and Hogg summed up the year's work in as few phrases. For 1831 he wrote: Admitted 340, cured 184, relieved 103, died 10, remaining 43. His accounts were equally sparse, showing cash received, expenditure on advertising, rent, drugs, printing, bottles and trusses and the apothecary's salary of £12 a year. Income and expenditure balanced at around £80.

The subscribers were permitted to nominate for treatment members of the "industrious poor" in proportion to their contributions. In 1809 subscribers could recommend two patients for a half-guinea, five for a guinea, and 11 for two guineas. The minutes made no reference to the 1839 smallpox epidemic, no doubt because infectious cases were beyond the scope of the dispensary and would have had to remain at home. There was an associated "cow pock dispensary" which did its best to guard against smallpox, and Hogg noted before the epidemic that 55 patients had been "gratuitously vaccinated".

During almost a century of existence the dispensary treated

over 30,000 patients, by any standard a splendid contribution. It passed into history in 1898 when the General Hospital opened, handing on a reserve fund of £1,005.

The General Hospital was built to meet a vital need as Kettering expanded. For years, serious cases went to Northampton or Leicester infirmaries by train, and the growing number of town doctors were constantly handicapped by the lack of an adequate hospital. They tried to start a fund for one in 1887 to mark Queen Victoria's golden jubilee, but could not raise enough interest. Inspiration came several years later from lay people able to catch the public imagination.

One was Mary Stockburn, eldest daughter of John Turner Stockburn, the leading townsman after the eclipse of the Gotch family when their bank failed. Like many daughters of the well-to-do, Mary felt called to help the poor. She trained as a nurse at Addenbrooke's Hospital, worked among crippled and mentally defective children at Canning Town, took charge of a Cripples' Workshops home and, as matron of a Women's Settlement in Essex, organised country holidays for East End youngsters. Returning to Kettering, she collaborated with Catherine Lindsay, the Rector's daughter, in founding the Nursing Association and became its first secretary. This put her in touch with afflicted families and, seeing the great need for a general hospital, she enlisted her father's aid. Stockburn was chairman of the Local Board — forerunner of the Council — and thanks to Mary's persistence he called a town meeting in 1891 at which a scheme for building a general hospital was launched.

Another prime mover was Thomas Iliffe, ironically the town's first tobacconist in days when no-one thought nicotine needed a health warning. He used his influence as a Local Board member to appeal for funds, which had to be raised entirely voluntarily. Money came in from all quarters, Stockburn giving £500 — a small fortune then — and by 1896 the organisers were within £2,000 of their target. They decided to achieve it with one gigantic five-day bazaar at the Victoria Hall in Gold Street, and such was the enthusiasm that £3,200 rolled in — enough to permit an immediate start.

The Duke of Buccleuch gave the five-acre site in Rothwell Road, the Kettering Iron & Coal Co. waived its right to mine the ironstone, construction went ahead to Gotch and Saunders' plans, and the building was opened on October 30, 1897, by "Bobby" Spencer (Lord Althorp), half-brother to the "Red Earl" Spencer, highly popular in Kettering as Liberal MP for Mid-Northants. He entered the Lords later as the sixth earl.

Originally the hospital consisted of the stone block with an imposing entrance standing high above Rothwell Road. There were three wards providing 23 beds of which four were for children, an operating theatre, offices and domestic departments. The contractors were paid £18,000, leaving £500 in the bank. In 1902 the first of many extensions increased the beds to 58.

As soon as the hospital got into its stride it was utilised to the utmost. In 1898-9 admissions were 179 — 75 men, 55 women and 49 children. The daily average of in-patients was 18.34 and their average stay 32.89 days. Amputations were breast 2, fingers 4, thighs 2 and toe 1. Excisions included bronchocele 1, diseased bone 4, inguinal hernia 1, hare lip 1, morbus coroe 1, rodent ulcer with skin transplant 1, sinus 1, tubercular testicle 1, tubercular joints 2, adenoids 5, exostosis of femur 1, foreign body in hand 1, growth on scalp 1, ingrowing toenail 2, birthmarks 3, polypus uteri 1, tonsils 3, tumours 3. Other operations were circumcision 5, dislocations 4, enterotomy 1, hysteropaxy 2, lithotripsy 2, osteotomy 3, ovariotomy 1, tenotomy 3.

Income for 1898-9 was £1,534, of which £700 came from collections in factories and workshops organised by secretary F. J. Woolley of Lindreas and treasurer F. Abraham of Bird & Son. Gifts were showered on the hospital — pheasants and rabbits from brewer Pickering Phipps of Rushton Hall, venison from the Duke of Buccleuch, strawberries from Mrs Phipps, hot-cross buns from Henry Barlow, a bathchair from solicitor C. W. Stringer, fruit and vegetables from harvest festivals, and flowers, toys, magazines, games, books, newspapers, frocks and pinafores from scores of well-wishers.

The hospital was run by governors, consisting of leading residents and the honorary medical staff of local doctors, who delegated their authority to a board of management. The Duke of Buccleuch was honorary president, J. T. Stockburn active president, and there were nine trustees. The governors came from several groups. Donors of £21 and upwards were governors for life; a gift of £1 1s entitled the benefactor to serve as a governor for one year; clergymen whose churches subscribed a guinea or more could serve for one year; any other body which raised a guinea could appoint a one-year governor; and all the honorary medical officers were governors for their term of office. The sums subscribed were worth vastly more then, before a century of inflation eroded the pound sterling.

All accidents or emergencies were admitted at any time of day or night, but non-urgent cases needed a letter of recommendation from a governor. Life governors could recommend one patient annually for each £21 they subscribed, and one-guinea governors could recommend one patient for the year their guinea covered. Subscribers of half a guinea could recommend a patient for examination or to receive appliances or dental aid. But recommendation did not guarantee admission, as applicants had to be vetted by one of the honorary medical staff to assess their degree of need. This ceremony was observed at noon each Friday. The doctors took turns at the duty, and each attended the patients he admitted until they were discharged.

Strict rules which eventually became by-laws governed the hospital. The salaried resident house surgeon was required to visit each ward and see each patient at least twice a day. He had to administer anaesthetics and assist at operations performed by the medical officers if required, but except in emergency he was forbidden to operate without the consent of the medical officer in charge of the case. He could not be absent for more than six hours without permission from the acting honorary medical officer or the board of management, and under no circumstances was he permitted to be away at night without sanction. The rules also required the matron to make her rounds of the wards twice daily.

Visits to patients, by ticket from the matron, were permitted only on Sundays from 2 to 3 pm and on Fridays from 2 to 3.30 pm. No patient was allowed more than four visitors on one day, and only two might be at the bedside at the same time. Things were no doubt different for private patients, who paid £4 4s a week upwards plus their doctor's fees. A glimpse of their comforts is provided by a rule that while they might have wines and spirits sent in, this was not part of the service and must be paid for as an extra.

The staff worked under stress during the 1914-18 war when many wounded soldiers received treatment. Extra funds were provided by the Government, and tented wards containing 60 beds were erected in the gardens. One burnt down in 1917. In addition there was, in London Road, a Voluntary Aid Detachment hospital, staffed by ambulance workers, with 94 beds. By the time the tented wards closed in 1919 the hospital beds had accommodated 972 military patients, and the VAD wards had treated 2,026.

By 1923 the work of the hospital had increased almost sevenfold compared with its early days, with 1,952 patients treated, of whom 1,182 were in-patients. Cases listed in the annual report typify hospital work at that time. Most frequent in the medical field were duodenal ulcer, gastric ulcer, marasmus (wasting disease) and rheumatoid arthritis, each with five patients. Among operations, 320 were for tonsils and adenoids, 102 dental, and others were appendix 51, circumcision 76, curettage of uterus 29, excision of birthmarks 19, laparotomy 15, inguinal hernia 11, foreign body in hand 10, with 29 operations for carcinomas and 33 for tubercular troubles. Of 932 surgical cases, 147 were accident victims. Only two admissions had valvular heart disease, and, except for one from Manchester, all patients were local. The motor age with its toll of travellers had yet to arrive. There were 103 medical cases.

Financial alarm bells rang for the first time. The year's income at £5,681 was £1,000 down because of a trade recession. Subscriptions, Hospital Week takings, and factory and workshop collections all fell, giving an adverse balance of £825, a new experience for the board of management. At the same time the needs of the hospital were increasing, and Dr J. D. Macintosh of Glasgow Infirmary, called in to advise, considered as absolutely necessary the provision of a nurses' home, more private wards, up-to-date X-ray equipment, and better accommodation for doctors.

This crisis was a watershed, forcing a financial review. So far the hospital had depended largely on splendid service given by volunteers too numerous ever to list, in addition to the honorary medical staff. Typical was Frank Berrill, manager of the Midland Bank. Before the hospital opened, all the preliminary meetings were held at his house, he served on the first committee, became honorary treasurer, and spent the next quarter of a century working for the hospital, besides helping the Nursing

Association and acting as treasurer for many organisations during the 1914-18 war. A grateful town gave him a motor-car, and followed it up with a player piano when he married Dr L. W. Dryland's sister Alice. In the same tradition was Mr H. T. Berry, the next manager of the Midland, who followed on as treasurer.

Among many other lay people who gave their services were Mr J. Stanyon, honorary secretary from 1906-21, succeeded in turn by Mr A. H. Bryan, head of shoe manufacturers Bryan & Son, and Mr G. W. Hague. Honorary radiographer was George Kirton, engineer at the Co-op Boot factory in Havelock Street. An amateur photographer with a scientific bent, he took on the work during the war and continued until the mid-twenties, visiting the hospital at call, developing the X-ray plates at home the same night and delivering them next morning.

But by 1924 the hospital was running into debt with a £1,000-a-year shortfall, and at the same time faced estimates of £2,000 for a new out-patient department, £2,000 for private wards, and £1,000 to furnish a new nurses' home. It was feared that the deficit would reach £2,000, and Wilfrid Mudd, chairman of the Hospital Week committee, appealed to the public to contribute at least £3,000. He was disappointed because of the continuing unemployment in the staple trades.

In these straits the management was forced to conclude that full-time professional administration specially directed to fund-raising was required. So Mr H. J. Lancaster, MC, was appointed secretary-superintendent, taking over at a time when things were difficult for hospitals everywhere. For the first time state control of hospitals was in the air but, despite their difficulties, the Kettering board of management was against it. They favoured retaining the voluntary system which secured for the hospital generously-given services of inestimable value, both lay and medical. Stating this policy they declared: "If the system falls to the ground, the expense will be enormous. Injury will be done to the welfare of the sick, to progress in research, and to training in the medical profession. The voluntary system is part of our hertitage."

A financial brainwave was urgently needed, and it came in the form of the Hospital Guild, a new system which greatly increased the regular income. The enthusiasm with which it was

The Duke of Buccleuch opened Warren Hill House, the new nurses' home, on May Day, 1926. With a big lounge for dances and excellent facilities, the building delighted the nurses. It stood in the midst of tennis courts, gardens and lawns on which marquees were erected for prizegiving days. The General Hospital then was run entirely by voluntary subscriptions and donations, and the crowd showed the enthusiasm of Kettering people. They dressed for the event, the women in hats, gloves, coats and costumes, and the men smartly turned out, some with silk hats. Today the gardens are car parks, and Warren Hill House is a medical department.   (General Hospital)

received and supported led the board rightly to believe that the financial future would be reasonably free from anxiety. The Guild started operations in 1927, and the need for it is shown by the figures. Although the income of £9,696 was the highest on record it did not cover costs, and the year's deficit of £801 put the hospital £3,088 in the red.

The Guild was open to all wage-earners and, in return for a weekly subscription, guaranteed free hospital treatment for the whole family. The subscription was 2d a week for a working adult and 1d for those under 18. In return the scheme covered the contributor, his wife, children of school age, and dependent parents and grandparents living with him. The benefits were summarised as medical attention, nursing and maintenance if an in-patient, and X-ray, massage and ultra-violet treatment if an out-patient. People too poor to contribute would be treated free. It was too good to miss and immediately attracted a wide membership.

Hospital Week gained a new lease of life. The monster fete and carnival provided all the fun of the fair in the Wicksteed Park. There were parades of decorated cars and lorries, air and water displays in which Northants Aero Club and Kettering Rowing Club co-operated, maypole and folk dancing by the schoolchildren, sideshows, entertainments, a dance in the pavilion and a big lakeside fireworks display. Philip Hague thought the Rowing Club's float was usually the best in the parade. One year they entered a comic fire engine, but the idea he remembered as a sensation was a stage coach with mettlesome 'horses' which swept from side to side, scattering spectators lined four or five deep on either side of the road. The annual cost of running the hospital rose to £11,597 but, thanks to the Guild and the volunteer fund-raisers, there was no more lamenting over finances.

By 1933 the management was sufficiently confident to float a £10,000 scheme for a new operating theatre, two medical wards, kitchen improvements and more bedrooms for nurses. The theatre opened in 1934, the X-ray department was re-equipped and new facilities established for sunlamp treatment, massage, radiotherapy, electrical diathermy, and improvements to ear, nose and throat treatment. There were now 100 beds, and the hospital's high standards earned it recognition from the

General Nursing Council as a training school.

In 1935 approximately 1,500 in-patients and 3,000 out-patients received treatment, and running costs had risen to £15,000. The medical staff, all honorary, consisted of five medical officers, five assistant medical officers, one anaesthetist, one specialist surgeon, one consultant urologist, one ophthalmic surgeon, one aural surgeon, one orthopaedic surgeon, one radiologist, one pathologist and one dental surgeon, with a nursing staff of matron, assistant matron, sister tutor, seven sisters, 30 nurses and three masseuses, plus 27 maids, three porters, three gardeners, the secretary-superintendent and three clerks. Patron was the Duke of Buccleuch, president Stephen Schilizzi of Loddington Hall, chairman Fred Tebbutt, vice-chairman Tom Seddon, and honorary treasurer R. P. Davies.

The 1930s were notable for many generous gifts. Vincent Mobbs gave £3,000 to be spent over three years. Alan Timpson gave £5,000, then doubled it, enabling a new boiler house, central heating plant and laundry to be added in 1938. In 1939 the £25,000 Cave Block was erected, made possible by a legacy of £12,000 from Walter Cave who kept an off-licence in Bath Road and left almost all his estate to the hospital. He had no close relatives, and though for some years a semi-invalid he had never received hospital treatment. The block, opened by the Duchess of Gloucester in 1941, included new casualty, physio-therapy and X-ray departments, a chapel, mortuary, rooms for the maids and a new children's ward furnished by Mrs Alan Timpson in memory of her parents, Charles and Ada Jane Rutherford of Liverpool.

Some of the many other benefactors and friends are com-memorated by the Prince William post-graduate centre and wards named after the Buccleuch and Spencer families, Dr Pretty, matron Agnes Jackson, Mr A. M. Lee, and Dr Frank Radcliffe.

There were small gifts without number, for it was an eleventh commandment that the people of Kettering should support their hospital. Keeping it financially sound was everyone's responsibility. Some people arranged sizeable donations or legacies, while those who could only manage small sums contributed to collections and other efforts, perhaps giving the "hospital number" (44) when they bought things at the Co-op, so donating their dividend. Gardeners grew extra vegetables for the hospital, especially potatoes, which they wheeled up Rothwell Road hill in sacks balanced on crossbars of bicycles. Other enthusiasts worked voluntarily in the hospital gardens or helped in the wards.

Raising money gave a cultural stimulus to the district. Rivalling one another in creative fun, towns and villages held fetes, sales, concerts and shows for the hospital, often attracting stars to figure in the programmes. Kettering Hospital Sports were famous, drawing 5,000 people to Northampton Road recreation ground to see athletes from all over the Midlands. Businesses entered expensive and time-consuming displays for processions and carnivals as a matter of honour, and after big events the heads of firms would turn out and walk round with spiked sticks picking up litter from the area.

Unusual gestures recall the times. One donation made anonymously in 1924 was "To commemorate October 30". That was the day of a Conservative election victory which returned Stanley Baldwin to No. 10 Downing Street in place of Ramsay MacDonald.

A small boy, Lester Hope of Cottingham, went to see his brother Tom who had been hurt in a motor accident, and found the hospital needed eggs. He spent three days walking round visiting friends who had hens, collecting new-laid eggs. The matron was amazed when he turned up at the hospital with 360! The nurses had no wireless, so *Evening Telegraph* readers clubbed together and bought one for £30. When the nurses tuned in, they were welcomed over the air by the announcer.

Mr G. W. Jackson from the Royal Albert Infirmary, Wigan, served as secretary-superintendent, and in retirement at Bishop's Stortford in his 89th year had happy recollections of the 1930s. The hospital then maintained a very close link with the public through a daily bulletin issued to the *Evening Telegraph* which gave news of admissions and patients' progress. He remembered that the egg collections which supplemented the efforts of the hospital's own hens were so thorough that in Desborough, for example, parties went from door to door asking for eggs. Fruit and vegetables were produced in quantity in the hospital gardens. He recalled local doctors attending their own patients in the medical, surgical, maternity and children's wards, and the generosity of townspeople in supporting the Guild and fund-raising efforts.

Dr John Notley, living in Cornwall, has happy memories too: "In the early 1930s, Kettering General was really a good cottage hospital staffed by some of the general practitioners who were helped by specialists from Northampton, Leicester and London. The business side was dealt with by a management committee mostly from the business fraternity. I remember Alan and Bea Timpson were leading people on it.

"The original building faced the road, and one entered the front door up a flight of steps. There were two wards, for male and female patients, and the operating theatre was on the right of the front door. The children's ward and X-ray department were down a corridor to the left, and there was also a block of private beds. Bea Timpson had a great deal to do with setting up the children's ward, which was ruled by a formidable but most efficient sister — Sister Moralee. She was a great personality, marvellous with the children who adored her, and respected by the medical staff. The click of her heels coming down the corridor was unmistakable.

"The real star of the consultant staff was Sir Gordon Gordon-Taylor, who I believe was persuaded to come by Dr Pretty. He was all that one could imagine in a London specialist — tall, handsome, with exquisite manners to everyone, and a brilliant surgeon. To watch him operate — I often had to assist him — was like watching the hands of a master musician. Then he left for the war and was posted a rear-admiral. He had already served in the First World War, finishing as a brigadier-general.

Dr Notley retired to Cornwall. This snap shows him taking a rest in the garden of his house, Leat Farm, near Yeolmbridge.

"Mr Holman from Northampton became the consultant surgeon. He was a very good surgeon, a quiet man, completely dependable. Mr Kendall from Leicester was the ear, nose and throat surgeon. He could be great fun and was most hospitable. I remember going to lunch with my wife and my second son Charles, who had a voracious appetite. Nick Kendall christened him 'Charlie Hollowlegs'. Dr Robert Watson from Northampton was gynaecological and midwifery specialist. He was an Ulsterman with a tremendous capacity for hard work who did not suffer fools gladly.

"As his registrar at Kettering, responsible for the day-to-day treatment of his cases, I had a lot to do with him and more than once had to suffer his sharp tongue. I had a great respect and affection for him, and we really got on well together. There was a consultant physician, but for the life of me I cannot recall his name. I remember him as a very nice man, always ready to help and explain things to us. I think that in those days all pathological specimens had to go for examination to Northampton Hospital. It was not until the National Health Service that we had a laboratory of our own.

"As for the staff, the only one I remember — and who could forget? — was matron Agnes Jackson from Burnley, appointed in 1935 from the Central Middlesex County Hospital where she was assistant matron. Agnes was a wonderful woman, and we all loved her. She was a great organiser, and friendly towards everyone. The nurses used to entertain the medical staff to dinner at Christmas. It was a great affair. The decorations were beautiful and the food and wine magnificent, but the NHS put an end to all that. The sisters were all very good and capable, but I am afraid that their names I can no longer recall."

Dr Notley was with the Dryland practice which produced one of the most remarkable records of service to the hospital. In 1938, Dr L. W. Dryland resigned as an honorary medical officer after 43 years. He had followed his father, Dr J. W. Dryland, who had served for 47 years. Another of Dr Notley's colleagues in the practice was Dr Frank Radcliffe who later under the NHS specialised in accident and orthopaedic surgery at the hospital.

Dr John Deutsch, who joined Dr Shirkey during the war on demob from the army, remembered that consultants used to come from Northampton on a weekly basis, and besides Mr Holman were Mr R. O. Lee, Mr Banham, Mr Lawson, a surgeon from Leicester, and Dr Rosenthal, a medical consultant who had one of the first portable electrocardiographs and would take it for use in patients' homes. As there was then no pathology laboratory in the town, Dr Deutsch set up his own lab with the help of Mr Ross of Stewarts & Lloyds, Corby, who made and presented him with an incubator. He did a lot of pathology, blood tests and simple bacteriology until, with the NHS, the new pathology lab at the hospital was established with Dr Harry Voss as its head.

A distinguished administrator was Mr A. M. Lee, in business as a leather merchant in old Tanners Lane. He was first connected with the hospital about 1930, elected chairman of the board of management in 1939, following in the footsteps of Frank Mobbs, William Ballard and Frederick Tebbutt, and in 1948, after nationalisation, he became chairman of the management committee. His wise guidance and calm influence contributed much to the smooth running of affairs during the initial period of the NHS. I remember his preoccupied air when I met him one day during the run-up to the takeover. "I am having to go round the district and meet people who accuse me of robbing them of their local hospital," he said. "It's a big job explaining that they are not losing but gaining the great benefits of the new service." No problem was too small for him to look into, and he was known by everyone from surgeons to stokers.

Mr Lee made great efforts to secure a £700,000 major development scheme which was approved by the Ministry of Health shortly before he retired. This meant that the hospital would develop into a district general hospital and, when the time came, one of those who with colleagues shouldered the work of expansion was Dr Thomas Partington, the consultant physician. Born near Oldham, he trained at University College and St George's Hospitals, London, and graduated in 1938. He joined the RNVR and saw war service with destroyers in the Malta and Russian convoys, the invasion of Sicily and the Salerno landings. He was in a landing craft on D-Day, went to the Far East, and finished as a surgeon lieutenant-commander.

Appointed consultant physician to Kettering and Northampton general hospitals, he built up the medical departments and for nine years was the sole physician for the two hospitals. His ward rounds are remembered as formal and always including a

106

teaching element for nurses and junior medical staff. He never married and had few interests outside medicine.

His obituary in the *British Medical Journal* recorded that on retirement in 1976 he helped the Knights of Malta to set up a British hospital in Teheran, Notre Dame de Fatima. He ran the medical department there until the fall of the Shah of Iran forced the hospital to close. He was kindly, sincere and humorous, but had a fiery temper when roused. His last years he spent on his own at Cheltenham, midway between members of his family to whom he was devoted, entertaining his visitors with lavish and painstaking hospitality. He died on Christmas Day 1988, aged 75.

Hospital discipline in the days of the old-fashioned matron is usually spoken of with emotions ranging from a healthy respect almost to awe. I have been fortunate to receive a first-hand account of life under two matrons between 1923 and 1930 from Mrs Marjorie Wright who joined Kettering General Hospital as a probationer nurse when she was 17. Her maiden name was Neale, and she was brought up in Boston where her father was a blacksmith and wheelwright. She always wanted to be a nurse and to go for training at the Middlesex Hospital where her aunt, Marjorie Tooke, was a nurse and had been gold medallist of the year.

This idea did not please her father. He regarded London as a wicked city and refused to let Marjorie go there, but he approved of Kettering when her mother noticed an advertisement for probationers. Marjorie wrote to the matron, was accepted on the strength of her letter, and the hospital sent patterns and material so that her uniform could be made up by a Boston dressmaker. Then Marjorie set off for Kettering with her possessions in a trunk. It was a day's journey by rail, as she had to change stations at Peterborough, go on to Manton and change trains to come to Kettering.

On arrival she met matron Kirkpatrick for the first time, and found her a rather overpowering personality in a navy-blue high-necked uniform with a floating-handkerchief cap and a service medal, as she had been an army nurse. There were 25 nurses and Marjorie shared a room on the first floor with two others. The probationers wore light blue dresses with white caps and aprons, white collars, cuffs and belts, stiffly starched, and black

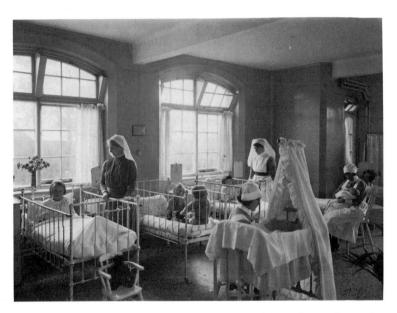

The children's ward in the 1920s. Matron Kirkpatrick stands on the left, sister Lowry is in the background, nurse Jones sits with a baby on her knee, and nurse Marjorie Neale is in the foreground. Photographer Charles Speight posed her looking into a cot, but there was no baby because the ward was in quarantine and not accepting patients. One of the children had developed an infection and been taken to Rockingham Road Hospital. The tablet on the wall records the gift of the Mabel memorial cot. (Marjorie Wright)

shoes and stockings. They had square-bibbed aprons, while the staff nurses wore round bibs.

Breakfast for the day nurses was at 8 a.m. to be on duty at 8.30 a.m. until 8.30 p.m., with two hours off during the day. The night staff had breakfast at 8 p.m. to be on duty at 8.30 p.m. until 8.30 a.m., with two nights off per month. There was one half-day a week and one whole day off a month. Holidays were a fortnight each year. And the food? — ''We were always hungry. The meals were fine for the day nurses but not so appetising on night duty, when the meat usually seemed tough, and the main course might be a pie dish of tripe and onions.''

Training to pass the SRN exam was in the hands of the sisters, who were kind but very strict. The probationers received evening lectures from the doctors, which they had to write up for check-ing by the sister tutor. Often they could not finish writing by lights out and had to add the final touches by retreating to the bathroom where there was always a light. Part of the training was for third-year nurses to go two at a time for six months' general experience on the medical wards at Northampton General Hospital, looking forward to the change of scene which put them within reach of the Northampton theatres. Exams were at the end of the first year, the final after four years, and then the hospital's own exam. After passing out, the probationers could join the staff as state registered nurses.

There was a change of matron while Marjorie was there. The new one, Miss L. A. Waterer, proved very strict and ruled the hospital. For her rounds everything had to be just so, beds precisely made, covers exactly right and pillows level. Redesigned uniforms were mauve and white check dresses for the probationers, mauve and white stripes for the staff nurses, and plain mauve for the sisters, all worn with white shoes and stockings, a source of much vexation in muddy weather.

In those days everything depended on good nursing as there were none of the modern drugs. Pneumonia had to be treated with poultices and tepid sponging to bring down the patient's temperature. Leeches were used if, for example, a patient had a poisoned arm, and there was only a tiny laboratory for tests. Frequent cases were burns from industry, broken bones, and operations on children for tonsils and adenoids.

Marjorie loved theatre work and assisted at many operations. From the beginning she was not affected by witnessing surgical procedures: "You could not think about yourself, as your whole attention was concentrated on the poor patient whom you were trying to help." Operations, unless unusually difficult and requiring a specialist, were carried out by the town general practitioners, who usually worked in pairs. On duty at each operation were the theatre sister, theatre nurse, and a nurse from the ward. The anaesthetic, applied by mask, was chloroform first, followed by ether and oxygen.

"We looked up to the doctors, who were marvellous surgeons," Marjorie says. "They were helped by specialists from Leicester and Northampton, among whom I remember Mr Lawson and Mr Carter. The eye specialists were Mr E. H. Harries-

Jones and later his son-in-law Mr S. G. H. Humfrey who was a county cricketer, and Mr Symonds, the Gold Street jeweller, came in to test for spectacles. Mr Padbury from Bedford ran the X-ray department with the help of the resident physiotherapist.''

Doctors Pretty and Tolputt introduced dissection of the tonsils instead of using a guillotine, which reduced the bleeding. Many little children had to undergo mastoid operations, and Marjorie found these harrowing as the wound had to be plugged and dressed with gauze. One particularly sad case was a little girl who was feeding a pet donkey when it suddenly bit her, inflicting a dreadful facial injury from which she died. Looking back, Marjorie recalls another occasion when as a young nurse she was upset. She was handed an amputated leg to take to the porter for incineration and, although it was swathed in towels, she realised as she carried it just how much the loss would mean to the patient.

Theatre routine included standing by to mop the brows of the surgeons, sterilising dressings under steam pressure, and disinfecting the theatre with Lysol and Condy's fluid.

There was plenty of enjoyment for the young nurses. They had tickets for the cinemas and big social events, and Christmas was always a splendid time. There was a lovely dinner for the patients with the surgeons carving, decorations, and relaxed rules with visitors free to come and go. After a new nurses' home was opened by the Duke and Duchess of Buccleuch the sitting room had a big open fireplace at each end, and dances were held there with Pat Thornton's band and the Richardson Players.

Marjorie Neale is centre. They were smiling at the news that Paul Taylor was to instal a wireless in the nurses' home. Marjorie's colleagues are, from left to right, nurses Thompson, Tonge, Taylor and Franklin.

(Marjorie Wright)

There were social distinctions, and Marjorie recalls stern words from the matron after she discovered that the house surgeon had taken a sister and some nurses — one of them Marjorie — to the Northampton variety theatre. Dr Pretty poured oil on troubled waters, pointing out that the young house surgeons, who stayed for about a year, had lonely lives and must be allowed some relaxation.

Marjorie became staff nurse in charge of the private block, relief night sister, and then sister of the children's ward. She met her future husband at the hospital. One day, shoe manufacturer Nick Wright came to see a colleague, Charles Mobbs, and brought a bunch of grapes. "Have a grape," he said to Marjorie, meaning her to help herself to plenty, but she took just one in accordance with the invitation. After many years of married life in Kettering, they moved to the old school house in Corby, and when Nick died Marjorie found a touching poem he had written for her. It recalled their first meeting and how their life together had begun with just one grape.

Dr Pretty used to say that when he came at the turn of the century the hospital was run by four doctors — Allison, Drake-Lee, L. W. Dryland and J. P. Roughton, who were all honorary surgeons and gave their time, knowledge and skill to save life entirely without payment. He and Dr Tolputt were elected assistant surgeons and, on his first day, Dr Pretty did 11 operations. To him the hospital owed the perfected tonsils operation, the first Ceasarean, more skilled help headed by Sir Gordon Gordon-Taylor, and the idea for the first operating block.

In 1952, things at Kettering still resembled the 1930s, and Pamela Harker who came in that year could say she was glad she'd seen the old days. She became senior ward sister on Lilford C when Warren Hill House was still a nurses' home: "It had a lovely lounge downstairs with a fire. There were tennis courts to play on in the evenings, and at the back of the house, now the car park, were gardens for the staff and patients.

"The gardeners were wonderful — they grew all the vegetables for the hospital. Prizegiving was a big occasion, with two marquees on the lawn, one for the prizegiving and the other for tea. There was much more friendliness among the nurses, as living-in we got to know one another well. In fact, we knew all the other nurses and the doctors, porters, domestics and telephonists. Titles used in those days were matron, home sisters and housekeepers. In those times, after say an appendix operation, a patient would be kept in bed for ten days. Now, after major surgery, you are up next day to prevent thrombosis and chest infections.''

As always, in the 1930s the hospital was constantly dealing with life-or-death potential tragedies of which the stories have been handed down in families with gratitude, especially in cases of difficult childbirth or other emergencies demanding urgent treatment. Volunteers were mobilised at a few moments' notice to give blood transfusions while specialists, family doctors, nurses and anxious friends strained every nerve on the patients' behalf. In return, the townspeople spared nothing in their efforts to maintain and improve an institution of which everyone was proud.

Several people have told me about their stay in hospital 60 years ago. Their stories are on the lighter side, but well illustrate the hospital atmosphere in those days.

Kitty Wiseman of Norwich (née Woodward of Kettering) when aged 17 developed appendicitis and was sent immediately to hospital by Dr Pretty at nine o'clock at night. She was conveyed in the town's only ambulance by Walter Dyson and another St John man who lifted her into a canvas carrier for transport downstairs. At the hospital door she was transferred to a trolley and wheeled straight into the operating theatre where Dr Pretty was scrubbing up ready to begin. Kitty was placed on the operating table next to a trolley laden with the surgical instruments to be used, which she found interesting to say the least! For the anaesthetic, Dr Pretty's assistants gripped her wrists in case she tried to fight off the mask which was placed over her face. Her time in bed after the operation was for a fortnight in hospital followed by a further week at home.

On other occasions painful moments came when she had a quinsy lanced, and when two septic toenails were removed. The quinsy was easy after she managed to open her swollen mouth, but the toenails were whipped off by Dr Pretty without anaesthetic. Kitty brought this on herself. Picked at 14 for the High School hockey first team she wanted to look smart, so borrowed a pair of the latest-style boots from Muriel Foster. The boots were too small and caused septic toenails along with considerable heartache when Kitty was rebuked by gym mistress Miss Prentice for playing below her standard.

In 1922, Phil Martin of Rothwell had an operation for the repair of a hernia. He was eight, and admitted for the same purpose was a Rushton boy, Charlie Essam. It was a Sunday afternoon and the ward staff started to make preparations for operations next day: "We had no tea, were put to bed and given doses of castor oil. At 5.30 next morning the night nurse woke me to give me an enema. It was painful; nothing much happened and I got the impression that she did not know what she was doing.

"Charlie and I were not given breakfast. A rather severe lady, whom we came to know as the ward sister, painted our tummies with iodine. We were told that when Dr Pretty was ready to operate an electric bell would ring and we would be taken to the theatre. I had never been to a theatre, so I asked whether it was anything like the pictures. I was told it was, and we might see Charlie Chaplin. However, the bell did not ring, and a nurse came to say that Dr Pretty had a septic finger and there could be no operations. We spent several days as walking patients until the doctor was ready. On the day, he came to the ward and spoke to us just before our operations, making some quip about labels pinned on to our theatre gowns to ensure that there would be no mix-up.

"The operations proceeded satisfactorily, but no Charlie Chaplin. Afterwards we spent four weeks recuperating. There were about 20 children in the Frank Berrill ward, a fair proportion to have adenoids removed. Family visiting was allowed for an hour in the afternoons on Friday and Sunday, and the fruit, cakes and sweets which the visitors brought were collected and, in theory, shared out as dessert after dinner. Some of the children complained that they never saw the things their parents brought. The food was meagre and unappetising and I was always hungry. Whenever I got a quarter of an apple or orange as dessert I used to eat the pips.

"Charlie and I got bored and homesick, but we had a pleasurable visit from Mr Rumbold, standing in for the Rector of Rushton who was on holiday. He brought us a Jules Verne story each. Charlie had *Five Weeks in a Balloon* and mine was *Round the World in Eighty Days*. It was very kind of Mr Rumbold as he didn't know me. A less pleasurable visit was from my parents. I had broken a thermometer and was told that they would have to pay for it. I was apprehensive but, of course, they paid without question.''

Reg Tailby had an unusual experience when 12. He was referred to the hospital by Dr Tolputt for treatment by Dr Roughton. He had just lost his father and, as his mother was left with four children and a young baby, he went to the hospital alone and told the nurses that Dr Tolputt had sent him.

"It was 1916, just after some of the worst battles of the Great War, and the gardens were covered with marquees filled with wounded soldiers in hospital blue uniforms. The medical and nursing staff were completely stretched, but in good spirits. Dr Tolputt's name was on my bed label though he was not a hospital doctor, and after a day or two of no treatment the sister asked if I would help by sterilising instruments. I agreed, and that became my job. I was then put on boiling eggs, hundreds of them every morning. I was quite the nurses' favourite.

"After about a month, sister said, 'We love you, but why are you here? You have a bed but no treatment, and you're not on the staff though working with us.' When I showed them my bed label the penny dropped — I should have been listed as Dr Roughton's patient. The error was corrected. Dr Roughton examined me and said I would be on Tuesday's operations list. When the day came I was starved and put in a long white gown. At 5.30 pm, with me very hungry, Dr Roughton came, looking exhausted after his day's work. He looked me over, then said, ''I don't think it matters much — you can go home.' So ended my month's working holiday at KGH.

"My connection with the hospital did not resume until the NHS took over in 1948. I became a member of the first management committee, serving for over 20 years, and was chairman for the three Kettering hospitals for five years. As it could not be done officially I initiated my own committee to appeal for a nurses' recreation centre. I was chairman, Paul Seddon (later Kettering Health Authority chairman) was vice-chairman, and other members were Alan Everard, Bill Hubball, Sydney Andrews and Fred Banks. That was one of the things I am proud to have fathered.''

Under the NHS, Kettering became the acute general hospital for the district, supplying operating theatres, wards and all support services for a population of 170,000. To begin with there were eight hospitals in the 11 towns, providing 1,015 beds. The hospitals were gradually reduced to four, while the general hospital was expanded from 131 beds in 1948 to 600 in 1988, giving a total for the district of 987 beds. The number of patients dealt with increased from 2,435 in 1948 to 30,726, plus 3,944 day cases for simple surgical treatment with no need to stay overnight.

The hospital service by 1988 had become one of the largest employers with 3,769 on the payroll throughout the district, of whom 2,057 were nurses. The population served has increased to 250,000, and the budget has risen from £256,908 in the first NHS year to £31,662,000.

I wonder what the 1927 treasurer Wilfrid Mudd would say to that?

THE DISTRICT NURSES

I once heard someone say: "Angels don't have wings — they wear blue uniforms and ride bikes. They're called district nurses." People who have been seriously ill or have had to see a loved one suffer will agree with that. A word from the doctor, and a nurse would trundle round the corner on her bike twice a day, magically easing pain, fixing dressings, setting things to rights and helping to banish fear. Yet only a century ago there were no trained nurses to help in people's homes.

Organised nursing began in Kettering after Florence Nightingale's revelations about the Crimean military hospitals awakened wide concern for the welfare of all sick and injured people. Returning to England, she was presented with £50,000 in recognition of her work for the wounded, and at once established a training school at St Thomas's Hospital to prepare district nurses for work in London. She was joined in the task by William Rathbone, a merchant whose wife had died from tuberculosis, leaving him with five young children. During her illness he had engaged a nurse, trained as far as was possible in those days, and saw how much difference her help made in his home. He began to realise the misery caused by illness in the wretched dwellings of the poor, and was inspired to finance a training school for nurses at Liverpool Infirmary.

Until then such home nursing as there was had been done by good-hearted women, often with no training and only rule-of-thumb experience, and in any case it was out of the question for poor families to afford help. William and Florence recognised the tremendous need for trained nurses and set a pattern for the establishment of nursing associations. They founded associations in London and Liverpool, recruiting as nurses girls of good education and background, and the Metropolitan and National

Nursing Association was formed as the professional authority. All nurses under its aegis had a year's hospital training, three months on a district under a superintendent, and eventually training in maternity work.

The scheme was assured of success when Queen Victoria gave it her blessing. To mark her golden jubilee in 1887 the women of England raised £80,000 to present to her. They commissioned a gold and diamond necklace as a personal gift, and the Queen requested that the remaining £70,000 should be used to found a trust for training district nurses. She allowed the association to change its title to the Queen Victoria Institute of Nurses, shortened to the Queen's Nurses. District associations became affiliated when they reached the required standards.

In Kettering some nursing for poor families had been financed by industrialist J. T. Stockburn, but the need was such that public funds were also required. In 1891 a group of ladies met to consider founding a nursing association. Mary Stockburn and Catherine Lindsay volunteered as secretary and treasurer, arranged an inaugural meeting, and Kettering District Nursing Association was launched at the Cross Keys with Dr J. W. Dryland as president and a committee of 20.

They appealed to the town for enough money to establish a headquarters, pay the salaries of two nurses, and purchase supplies and appliances. Families, clubs, factories, shops, societies and companies were asked to help, and Miss Lindsay at the Rectory, Miss Stockburn at the Mission House, and Miss Knibb in Huxloe Place opened books for cash and promises. Familiar names crop up in the early records. Mr C. T. Cooper was elected secretary, and Miss Toller, Miss Mursell, Mrs Percy Grundy and Mrs Northern were on the first committee. Miss Nellie Timpson, put on the committee in 1900, became secretary in 1913 and was still vice-president in 1941. Mr G. Page served on the executive for over 46 years. A room in Havelock Street was rented as the first headquarters, soon vacated for a house in Montagu Street, run by a housekeeper. Superintendent nurse Miss White and probationer Miss Watts were the first staff.

The committee were surprised when some prejudice against the association became evident, and took time to die down. A fund-raising leaflet had tactlessly stated that the nurses were to help the "sick poor", and few people cared to be thought of as dependent on charity. The leaflet continued in similar vein, emphasising social divisions:

"Families are often not skilled in the art of nursing, are without necessary appliances, and are unaware of preventable sanitary evils surrounding the patient which may impede or prevent recovery. Frequently, in acute cases, removal of the patient would be fatal. Other cases, under medical direction and with the assistance of trained nurses, can be considerably alleviated without requiring the poor to leave their homes.

"The work of a visiting nurse among the sick poor differs from that of a hospital nurse. In addition to personal attention to the patient the nurse is responsible for the condition of the sick room, and may have to sweep a floor, light a fire, and prepare nourishment for such as are helpless and unattended. Two visits daily generally suffice to perform the most essential skilled services and for the medical orders to be carried out. The association does not undertake to supply resident night nurses, and nurses are not empowered to provide nourishment from the funds of the association. District nurses are not allowed to receive presents of money from their patients. Those who feel gratitude will show it best by contributing to the funds."

The nurses had to be total abstainers, the association was non-denominational, and no help could be given to infectious cases or, in the early days, to maternity patients.

Removal of patients from their homes would have been to the sick ward provided by the Guardians at the workhouse, which though described by a contemporary writer as "the beautiful hospital at Kettering Union" was dreaded because having to go there was proof of one's poverty, then almost a deadly sin.

The plight of one patient was glimpsed in the first annual report. A poor woman recovering from confinement had a painful breast abscess. She was too ill to leave her bed, and could do nothing for her newborn baby or her five other children. Her only help was from the nurses who washed her and her baby, dressed the children, swept and dusted the room, cleaned the hearth, carried ashes and dirty water downstairs, did everything else that was needed, and left the family bright and comfortable until evening when a second long visit was necessary. Similar descriptions could have been included in subsequent reports to show the value of the service, but they are absent. Perhaps such reality was not welcome reading in the comfortable drawing rooms of the subscribers.

The original staff were soon succeeded by a new senior nurse, Miss Marshall from Leicester, and a fresh probationer, Miss Bodley from Winchester Hospital. During the year they made 2,567 visits to 179 cases, of whom 98 became convalescent and 34 died. In 1893, a year of mixed fortunes, the nurses first passed the Queen's Institute tests, and Kettering Association became affiliated to the Institute, one of the first in the county to achieve this status. Then a typhoid epidemic ran the two nurses off their feet, and a third nurse had to be engaged. The disease was caught by 95 people and, between mid-August and mid-November, typhoid patients alone needed 4,394 visits, while other cases demanding attention during the year were abscesses 35, bronchitis, pleurisy and asthma 24, fractures, injuries and operations 22, obstetrics 22, influenza 13, burns and scalds 10, constipation and obstruction 10, ophthalmic 5, cardiac 5, cancer 4, acute rheumatism 3, syphilis 3, hysteria 2, kidney disease 2, and single cases of colic, jaundice, tetanus, convulsions and dropsy.

In 1899 the town population had grown by 10,000 since the association was founded, and the nurses were foot-slogging along many new streets. To the rescue came cycle dealers Peter Hunt and Harry Taylor, providing the nurses with their first bicycles and teaching them to ride. By 1903 over 600 subscribers were contibuting £230 a year, but this was not enough and the first factory collections were started, supplemented with collecting boxes in private houses. Competitive street totals were published, which proved a powerful spur to generosity.

In 1905 an inspector from the Queen's Institute would not pass the headquarters as adequate. The association occupied a whole house, but the nurses had increased to five and two slept out in lodgings, not considered convenient for speedy contact. A move was made to roomier quarters in Tennyson Road. In 1910 a little-known charity received a brief mention in the report. This was the Kettering Blanket Loan Society, which for years had done its best to see that sick people with little money were at least kept warm. Realising that the nursing association could take over its work, the KBLS handed over blankets and cash, and disbanded. Cases that year rose to 504 and visits to 11,737.

During the 1914-18 war, services had to be reduced because

of a shortage of nurses in a town which did its full share of caring for the wounded, but adequate cover was maintained. After the war the problem of lack of money returned, and in 1919 the association was forced to break with tradition and introduce charges for those who could pay. Many people were better off than their parents were when the movement was founded, and it was felt that patients could meet part of the expense according to their means. Pensioners and 'parish cases' — the very poor — would still be treated free.

A great improvement was the appointment of a nurse-midwife, which at last opened up the wide field of maternity work. By 1922, 37 maternity cases needing 745 visits were among 285 patients receiving 8,580 calls during the year. Charges to patients, however, raised only 11% of the total costs of £650, and fees were standardised at midwifery 5s, maternity 15s, general nursing from 2d to 8d a day, and from 2s 6d to £1 for a nurse preparing for and attending an operation, all subject to adjustment according to the patient's circumstances.

Maternity cases increased in 1924 to the point at which an additional midwifery nurse had to be engaged, but by 1927 the nurses were under such strain that the report stated frankly that they had reached the limit of their physical strength, yet still felt that they were not doing justice to the work. This pressure was all too evident in 1928 when visits rose to 22,057 — the largest total yet — the accounts were overdrawn despite record income, and the association had outgrown its Tennyson Road headquarters, with three nurses on the premises and three in lodgings.

It seemed providential when Miss Christine Stockburn most generously presented the association with Belle Vue, a beautiful house in its own grounds off Broadway, in memory of her parents as the Stockburn Memorial Home, providing accommodation for the nurses, domestic staff and the office. The first superintendent, Miss Grigg, was appointed and the work was expanded to include caring for under-fives with measles, whooping cough, pneumonia and diarrhoea on behalf of the Council Health Department.

In 1933 a new appointment was that of a salaried organising secretary, Mr E. C. Bull. A provident scheme was started so that families could make regular payments entitling them to nursing when needed and, in the following year, improved finances paid for a four-bedroom extension to Belle Vue, with an additional bathroom and linen store. Sidney Loasby, also well known as the organist at the Parish Church, succeeded Mr Bull, and by 1938 the provident scheme reached a membership of 10,000 contributing £2,000 through collecting points at factories, offices, churches, social and political clubs, and private houses.

Miss Grigg retired and Miss Riddler took over in 1939, facing wartime conditions, the difficulty of obtaining nurses and midwives, and in 1941 a flu epidemic, plus the hazards of the blackout. Yet visits paid were 22,767, and they continued near this level until 1947 when, in its last year before combining with other services into the NHS, the association notched up 22,450 calls to 992 cases. The staff was Miss K. Morrison, superintendent, and seven nurses.

The final year ended with a £1,616 deficit, but in his notes Dr Drake-Lee felt that this was deliberate — the committee had "pushed the boat out" so that needed improvements could be made before they wound up 57 years of wonderful endeavour which brought blessings to thousands of people. This was the moment at which the doctor paid his tribute to those "angels on bikes":

"Through many years I have found the district nurses the salt of the earth, bringing comfort and healing to all classes in their own homes. They are a great boon to the patients and to the doctors, who know that their instructions will be carried out with meticulous care and cleanliness, the outcome of their special training. Before the motor-car the nurses made their visits cheerfully on foot or by bicycle in all weathers and at all hours, with never any talk of overtime. Nursing was their vocation and way of life, and we doctors and the public can never repay them for all their skill, kindness and devotion."

Today the nurses' traditions are exactly the same, but their way of life has changed. In former times they were often single and lived at the nurses' home, but now they are usually married and live with their families. They work in teams attached to the doctors' surgeries but are still based at the Stockburn Home, which houses the offices, a number of clinics and is the headquarters of the evening nurses. The number of community nurses serving the town of Kettering is now 43 — rather a change from the original two.

THE ST JOHN AMBULANCE

Until the later years of the last century there was an often astonishing indifference to the sufferings of sick and injured people. In some districts they were moved by road and rail with less care than goods and chattels, and the obvious need for skilled and compassionate handling inspired the Red Cross and the St John Ambulance Brigade to take the lead in improving matters. Reflecting public opinion, classes in first aid began at many centres in the 1880s.

At Kettering, Dr Daniel Drake-Lee held classes which were followed in 1886 by a course organised by Mr C. W. Lane, a solicitor who had been an active ambulanceman before coming to the town. Dr John Winter Dryland was the lecturer, and the students were mainly railwaymen who showed great keenness to qualify. These classes were among the first in the county and led, in 1893, to a town meeting at the Cross Keys which decided to set up an ambulance centre and to help in the formation of a Kettering Corps of the St John Ambulance. A committee of 39 people including the doctors was appointed, and founder-members of the Corps came forward from the police, fire brigade, gas company, railway and brewery.

At the same time a branch of the St John Ambulance Association was founded, which then, as now, looked after fund-raising, lectures, classes, public meetings and examinations, while the Corps consisted of disciplined Brigade members undertaking practical first aid, nursing, the transport of injured people, and first aid cover at public events, holding themselves ready to act in emergencies at any time.

As early as 1896 every policeman in the Kettering division had passed a first aid exam, some with marked success, and the Corps was doing admirable work at sports and other large gatherings, removing casualties to the Infirmary or by rail to Northampton and other hospitals, saving much suffering and helping injured people back to normal life. It was a busy year in which the Corps moved all the sick in the workhouse to the new Infirmary, helped the district nurses with heavy lifting, and set up four first aid stations in the town, two with wheeled litters given by the Working Men's Club and the Co-operative Society.

But all was not well. Regretfully the Association had to acknowledge that its work had been hampered and the members disheartened by lack of support. They had sent 300 letters to residents asking for financial backing, but the response was so poor that the money raised only just paid for the postage. The letters were followed up with a personal canvass but even that was miserably disappointing: "Members of the Corps, who are nearly all working men, received neither support nor encouragement, and were even left to pay expenses incurred in helping others," said the secretary. Charitably he assumed that Kettering had been asked to do too much at once, as appeals were also being made on behalf of the general hospital fund and the nursing association.

Where there's a will there's a way, and a new start was made with classes under doctors Dryland, Roughton, Allison and Lee, producing 231 men and 24 women qualified in first aid, and funding improved after a paid collector was appointed. By 1898 every factory of importance was equipped with an ambulance box supplied and maintained by St John, the number of fully equipped ambulance stations increased to eight, and 322 men and 86 women passed out as first-aiders. Uniforms were commissioned from the Co-op Clothing and Lovell & Brown. But all this was not achieved without occasional friction. Members attended Kettering Town football matches in case someone was hurt, but they were not appreciated and the Club was warned that the ambulancemen would be withdrawn unless they received better treatment and an apology from the trainer.

In 1899 the secretary happily reported that the town now realised its responsibility, apathy had been shaken off, and a horse-drawn ambulance costing £95 was in commission. This was a useful tool, as Wellingborough had found that its horse ambulance travelled 700 miles in the first two years. Northampton had a luxury vehicle built by Mulliners, but horses had to be hired from a transport firm which put the ambulance fourth on its list of priorities! Weddings and funerals had to be horsed first, then cabs for hire, and next the fire brigade, so that on a busy day injured Northampton people awaiting transport to hospital might well have opted out in favour of a glass-sided vehicle in the first group.

Calling out the Kettering horse ambulance cost 4s, and out-of-town journeys were 2s per return mile, plus a charge for attendants. This was cheaper than Northampton, which quoted a 10s call-out charge plus 3s a mile and lunch for the attendants if over eight miles. Besides the horse ambulance, litters, stretchers and first aid equipment, the Kettering assets included a skeleton used for anatomy classes which cost £3, and a bugle used for mustering members in pre-telephone days.

By 1909, brewer John Elworthy was president, town doctors formed the medical staff, and there was a strong committee of prominent people with Eustace Lane as secretary and Walter Dyson as storekeeper. Kettering Corps had divisions at Pytchley, Burton Latimer, Broughton, Rothwell, Rushton, Twywell and Woodford, and members organised a summer camp at Felixstowe. The churches were thanked for generous backing, and superintendent H. Raby was supported by first officer A. E. Linnell, sergeants J. Miller and C. W. Curtis, and corporals W. Groome and J. Jarman.

During the 1914-18 war, eight members of the Kettering HQ Division lost their lives when the *Royal Edward* was sunk in the Mediterranean. Every fit man joined up when the war broke out, and the nursing sisters under superintendent Mrs M. Farmer were called upon to help care for the wounded, undertaking a great deal of good work at the Voluntary Aid Detachment Hospital in London Road.

Northampton took delivery of its first motor ambulance, costing £700, in 1912, but Kettering had to wait until after the war when the Corps obtained a Napier which had seen service in France, given by the special constables, and a Ford on loan from the St John and Red Cross vehicle reserve. One was kept at Kettering and the other at Desborough. Transport committee members were chairman Tom Seddon, vice-chairman H. Curtis, secretary Charles W. Curtis, W. H. Baker, W. Whittlestone, A. E. Fox, police superintendent H. Tebbey, divisional superintendent W, Dyson, and Corps sergeant-major J. Miller.

By 1925, Kettering Corps had ten divisions numbering 200 men, with Corby, Geddington and the Midland Railway joining the list. Kettering HQ division was under superintendent Dyson and ambulance officers J. Liquorish and E. Claypole. Three nursing divisions — HQ, Cytringan, and the Co-op Clothing — under superintendents Mrs Willis, Miss Tansley and Miss Watson mustered 80 nursing sisters, there were divisions at Rothwell and Geddington, and a detachment at Corby. Boy cadets under ambulance officer W. Mandeville numbered 45, and there were 50 girl cadets under ambulance officers Miss Linnett and Miss Maule. Doctors served as divisional surgeons.

Members made personal sacrifices as part of their contribution to the life of the community. They were always at call to attend accidents or sudden illness, and formed rotas to cover sports and social events, staffing an ambulance room or tent. There was no remuneration, only out-of-pocket expenses, and members contributed to the cost of uniforms and rations when in camp. Official allowances barely met the cost of equipment, and in 1931 finances were so tight that one of the doctors suggested collecting contributions from street accident cases given first aid by the St John, but this was never implemented.

Inspections were gruelling and set a high standard. In 1937 the Corps paraded in Dalkeith Place and marched to the Wicksteed Park with the Salvation Army Band. After inspection they put on a practical drill in which members acted as casualties and were given first aid and bandaged by their comrades. There was then a further inspection by county officer C. W. Curtis, and the divisions dismissed after spending more than two hours in full uniform and equipment under a boiling sun.

The outbreak of war in 1939 brought great activity in training, with 55 classes in first aid and nursing. Students gained 1,245 certificates in that year, with other honours, and by 1941, when 1,732 people qualified, the total awards issued at the Kettering centre since 1893 totalled 7,429. In 1943 there was a quiet celebration to mark 60 years since the first ambulance classes in Kettering, and the golden jubilee of St John in the town. Work continued steadily until the foundation of the National Health Service and the gradual transfer of the main ambulance service to the authorities.

Princess Alice, Duchess of Gloucester, on a wartime visit to Desborough St John. With HRH are Council chairman George Turner, medical officer Dr W. E. Lock, his daughter Susan, the Marchioness of Exeter, County Commissioner Dr L. W. Dryland and County Superintendent (Nursing) Mrs Harvey Reeves.
Nurses (left to right), first row: Margaret Hart, Betty Essex, Doris Coe, Joyce Simmons, Rose Pentlow, Norah Marlow, Doris Simmons, Annie Fenton, District Nurse Chambers, Dorothy Groocock, Hilda Coe, Evelyn Blissett, Marjorie Daniels, Maud Pridmore, Margaret Dines and Mrs D. Chamberlain.
Middle row: Lizzie White, Mrs F. Walker, Joyce Timson, Ellen Smith, Roma Liner, Mrs D. F. Andrews, Dorothy Pateman, Mrs Baxter, Miss Berry, Yvonne Walker, Margaret Summers, Kathleen Gadsby and Isobel Watts.
Back row: Mrs Broomhead, Audrey Barnes, Mrs Kilborn, Dolly Bennett, Florence Bloxham, Mary Dines, Mrs Essex and Miss Green. Names from Ronald King, Howard Lewis, Rev. Melfyn Powell and Frank Roberts.

(St John Ambulance)

127

Of the many personalities who served, Walter Dyson is memorable not only because he so often turned out to accidents with the ambulance, but because his public work had so many facets. Brought up in King Street, he received a good start in public affairs from his father, a councillor and also named Walter. Father made shoes in Regent Street, and young Walter used to run to the shop as soon as he was released from Stamford Road School to help with end-of-day benchwork.

Leaving school, he got a factory job as a clicker and, in 1901, married his youthful sweetheart Lydia Saxby who had come from Irthlingborough to work at Wheelers the High Street jewellers. A fortnight later he was sacked because of a shortage of orders, but he walked round to the Kaycee clothing factory in Field Street and was taken on as a temporary hand. More than 40 years later he retired, having become head of the factory welfare services.

Walter's duties were so arranged that for much of the day he could turn out for the St John Ambulance to give first aid and take casualties to hospital. His interest in ambulance work began as a boy when a St John man lodging at his parents' home got him to act as a dummy for bandaging and the application of splints and slings. He joined the St John in 1904, worked up to divisional superintendent in 1924, corps superintendent in 1932, a serving brother in 1933, and an officer brother of St John of Jerusalem in 1954, collecting on the way the King George Medal for ambulance work, the life-saving medal, and a long-service medal after 40 of his 56 years' membership.

Many people owe their lives to Walter and his colleagues who, until the formation of the National Health Service, provided accident cover for 24 hours of every day. All the drivers were voluntary, giving on-the-spot first aid as well as transport to hospital when necessary. Funds came from firms' donations, gifts from well-wishers, factory collections, flag days and fetes, all arranged by St John members and friends.

Walter's house, just across the road from the factory, was an unofficial surgery. He kept a supply of emergency equipment always ready, as many people with injuries came knocking at the door for help. His daughter Eva, now Mrs Charles Starmer of North Walsham, remembers answering the door to a child with a dart stuck in her skull, whom Walter rushed straight to the hospital in his car. Eva says: "Without a wonderful wife who never sought the limelight he could not have accomplished these things. She was always in the background with a welcoming cup of tea. Many of the Kaycee girls came over when they weren't well, and there was always a cup of tea and a comfortable warm lie-down on the settee by the fire. It was marvellous that they lived to see their diamond wedding."

Another demanding field for her father was local government work. He was for 16 years a member of Kettering Urban Council, becoming chairman in 1938, then continuing on Kettering Borough Council and serving as mayor in 1949-50. He was made the borough's first freeman in 1956, the citation recording his fellow councillors' high regard for him and their appreciation of his long and distinguished service as a councillor and alderman, a county councillor, and a voluntary worker in the welfare services.

His work in the county brought him two unusual gifts. The officers and men of the Northamptonshire Fire Service so valued his efforts as chairman of the fire brigade committee that they made an inscribed dinner gong from the brass bell of one of the fire engines and presented it to him in 1951. He was a regular visitor to Tiffield Approved School, and was very proud of a glass case made by the boys to hold his scroll when he became a freeman of Kettering. Two Northampton hospitals recognised his work as a visitor. St Andrew's named a ward after him, and St Crispin's gave him its long-service medal.

More honours came from the fire service. He joined the Kaycee fire brigade in 1905, served 40 years and was its chief for 29 years, captaining it when it won the Lilford Challenge Trophy against 21 entries from seven counties. He judged at international contests, and the French Federation National des Sapeurs-Pompiers made him a member of honour, as did the Belgian Federation Royale des Corps de Sapeurs-Pompiers with a gold medal. Medals were presented by the Fire Brigades' Association for services rendered in 1944, for meritorious service in 1950, life membership in 1953, and from the International Fire Service for meritorious service in 1958.

The trombone was his favourite instrument. He owned three, played other instruments, joined in orchestras, conducted the Kaycee orchestra, helped Geddington Operatic Society who gave him a silver snuffbox, and on occasions was guest conductor of Kettering Salvation Army Band and Munn & Felton's. For years he took his auto-harp to the General Hospital on Christmas Day, playing for carols and delighting the children as Father Christmas.

The family holiday with Lydia, Eva, Noel and Vera was once a year to Gorleston, but he remained close to the job, as they stayed with another ambulance family whose father served turns on a hospital ship run by the Royal Mission to Deep Sea Fishermen, and their hosts paid return visits to Kettering. Walter's advice to the young was: "Do your job well, and cultivate a hobby that will give you an interest when you are old." He used to say "Ambulance work is my religion", and many of his hearers wished they had a practical religion to compare with his emulation of the Good Samaritan. A wonderful man, remembered with gratitude by many people for his inspiring cheerfulness, heartening competence and complete dedication to his town.

Another pillar of the Corps was cadet superintendent William Mandeville, who held the long-service medal with four bars for 35 years' continuous membership. During the 1914-18 war he was in France with the RAMC Field Ambulance Division, and his peacetime work with the boy cadets produced many experienced ambulancemen. As soon as they were old enough, his daughters Margaret and Gertie joined the girl cadets for training. Gertie says: "In the evening session we ended up being able to bandage ourselves from head to foot, all except the last hand. We looked like Egyptian mummies.

"A small cupboard with a pink glass door hung on the living room wall at our house, 4 Wellington Street. This held smelling salts, iodine, healing ointment, plasters and bandages. In my childhood our dinners were many times spoiled because someone would come for Dad's assistance to treat a cut, bruise or broken bone, and once a gruesome hand that had been squashed in mangle cogwheels. The ambulance people were very important in a community which had no emergency service to the hospital and few telephones. They helped willingly, with no thought of payment.

"One night a young man came who had fallen off his motorbike. Dad left him in the sitting room while he went to get some

In 1933, Kettering HQ Division of St John set a new record with 28 members holding the long-service medal. Here they are in the garden of Orchy Lodge, Dr Dryland's house in London Road.

Shown with years of service in brackets are (left to right), front row: Sgt E. W. Munn (23 years), Cadet Supt W. F. Mandeville (22), Ambulance Officer J. Licquorish (28), Supt E. Claypole (23), County Officer C. W. Curtis (28), County Commissioner L. W. Dryland, MRCS, DPH (37), Corps Supt W. Dyson (29), Corps Sgt-Major J. Miller (36), Pte A. Joyce and Staff Sgt W. Groome (both 28).

Middle row: Pte A. Issit (16), Sgt F. Wilson (27), Cpl M. Foster (21), Pte W. H. Brown (28), Pte W. Hankins, Pte W. L. Hewitt, Pte A. Brown and Pte G. Turner (all 17), Cpl F. Sweeting (25), and Sgt W. Woolmer (22).

Back row: Cpl A. Cullip (26), Pte H. J. Webb (19), Pte A. Percival (16), Cpl H. Brooks and Pte A. Lenton (both 17), Pte A. Coleman (27), Pte H. B. Wills and Pte F. H. Haynes (both 17).

(Evening Telegraph)

131

hot water from the kitchen. After first-class attention, he left. In the morning, Mother found her purse was missing. It contained all the money for our family holiday due to start the next day. I like to think that the young man was desperate enough to need it. Not many people resorted to stealing in those days.''

She remembered the first motor ambulance, a funny-looking van-type vehicle with big and obvious black mudguards, a high step to get in at the front, and an impressive horn to frighten people out of the way. The stretcher was placed awkwardly on the floor, and practice was needed to get it on board without tipping the patient off. The second vehicle, advanced by comparison, had dark one-way windows to prevent the curious from looking in, a first aid box, a water carrier, a rack for the stretcher, a seat for the ambulance officer beside the patient, and seats for other people who might need to travel. The emphasis was on minimum treatment and maximum speed to hospital.

On the nursing side, Miss Mary Cooper, who is a serving sister of St John, can look back with pride on a family link with the brigade covering 95 years. Her mother, Elsie Payne, was a founder member of Kettering HQ nursing division in 1897. She made nursing her career and in 1901 joined the staff of the Kettering Union, in earlier days known as the workhouse. It was the only refuge for poor people who were sick or aged and who needed nursing care.

The master, Mr Sattin, was an autocratic boss who lived on the top floor of the tower which was the central feature of the frontage in London Road. He retired to his rooms in the evening, and whenever he wanted one of the nurses he would place an oil lamp in his window — a signal for which they had to watch however busy they might be. Many times Elsie ran up the spiral stairs to see what he needed, and generally had to return to the ground floor and rush up again with something basic like a cup of coffee, a copy of the paper, or odds and ends Mr Sattin had left in his office.

Hedgehogs were kept as pets in the kitchen because they could be depended on to eat the cockroaches. Painted on the dining room walls were some first-class still-life pictures of items of food — fish, loaves, meat and fruit — all painted by a tramp who was a regular caller at the casual wards. Each tramp had a task to perform in return for his night's lodging, and Patrick, instead of chopping wood, was asked to paint another picture.

Elsie trained in London for midwifery, came back and married William Cooper, and their house in York Road became a casualty centre where Elsie could always be depended on for first aid. Mary, born in 1915, went to Miss Hitchman's school in the Victoria Hall and the church schools in Market Street and Market Place before she reached the Central School. As a girl guide she was attracted to first aid and joined St John, rising to divisional superintendent and a serving sister, completing 51 years' service. Most of it was in Kettering but part in Altrincham, where she moved for a time with William Timpson's staff when the office was transferred to the Manchester area.

Part of her early work at Kettering was ambulance duty at the Wicksteed Park during the summer. Her first case was a boy who wandered into the path of a tipper amusement which hit him behind the ear, almost severing it. Mary had him rushed to hospital, and the ear was saved. There were many other injuries and problems, usually due to people disregarding the park rules, falling or collapsing, but those who fell in the lake were cared for by the park staff who always had dry clothes ready.

When the war came, Mary was absorbed into the nursing staff at the General Hospital and then went on to do district nursing until 1946, cycling round in the blackout and having to find houses by feeling the numbers on the doors, perhaps attending a case at cottages off Pytchley Road and finding her next patient's address was in Blandford Avenue.

Nowadays she is still ready to help, but leaves major first aid jobs to younger people. She keeps busy with work for the Parish Church and running a club for many friends who worked at William Timpson's and meet regularly to remember old times.

There is less need for the St John now, for much of the work has been taken over by the NHS, which provides the ambulance service. On the other hand, there are first aid and nursing requirements which are better provided by a voluntary body, and local St John members are kept busy meeting these needs. They include first aid duty at public events, escorting invalids or infirm people who have to make journeys by car or public transport, and sitting with invalids or helping to care for them. Divisions in the northern area of the county are Kettering HQ,

Desborough, Rothwell, Burton Latimer, Thrapston and Corby, each with its own ambulance. During the Gulf War, they all stood ready to help receive and transport the wounded expected to arrive by air.

'Badgers', who enter for training at the age of six, are a new group which has joined the men, women and cadets who form the force. These very young entrants are in accordance with the present-day St John philosophy. Members are keen to spread first aid knowledge and expertise, and are working to interest schools so that all children can receive training in basic first aid.

THE GOTCHES

When the Gotches came to Kettering 250 years ago they found
a town of 3,000 people, depending on weaving and a market.
When they left two centuries later it had become a thriving
industrial borough of 40,000. Their influence transformed
Kettering. Through three generations they provided civic leadership, and they introduced the shoe trade. For their one great
miscalculation they made ample amends.

The full story of the family is being written by Christopher
Gotch, son of Laurence and grandson of Davis Frederick, who
both lived in Kettering. He was born in Kettering, lives in
London and has been researching trunks full of Gotch papers.
So far he has drafted 17 chapters of a book *Black Hats and
Hidden Voices*, sub-titled *Scenes from Provincial Life*, which
will include a great deal of new material about day-to-day affairs
in old-time Kettering. I am grateful to him for help with this
chapter, and look forward to the book which promises to be a
standard work on Kettering.

Originally the family name was Gowch, and in the 1500s they
farmed at Great Langton, Leicestershire. About 1740, John Gotch
moved south, found a wife at Rothwell, lived at Glendon, farmed
at Cherry Hall, attended the 'Little Meeting' (later Fuller), and
was buried in its graveyard when he died in 1784 aged 69. There
were three sons, Thomas, John and William. John had a butcher's
shop and his descendants found fame in Australia. William set
up as a shoemaker in Shoreditch, and Thomas stayed at home
to very good effect. Though unlettered, frail and complaining,
he was curiously forceful. In partnership with James Cobb he
began to manufacture boots and shoes in 1786, also tanning
and dressing the leather. No-one knows where the idea came
from, but his wife was a Walsall girl and her family may have

135

had shoemaking connections in Staffordshire.

At first Thomas Gotch lived in a stone house in High Street where the National Westminster Bank stands. He prospered, and in 1793 bought the house now known as Chesham House in Lower Street, living there and making it the headquarters of a business which became the largest bootmaking firm in the county, fulfilling military contracts through perilous times. All the making was done by outworkers who collected their leather and other materials, worked at their cottages as family units, returned a week later with the completed boots, were paid, and drew more supplies. They came from many miles around, and the busy scenes in Lower Street as horse transport, handcarts and people on foot gathered round the business wing of Gotch's house can be imagined.

Thomas and his wife, Anne Cooper, had 13 children, but only one survived, John Cooper Gotch. Anne always wrote to him as "My dear only son," and Thomas, though proud of his wife and his business, was particularly so of his son, whom he sent to Chesham to learn tanning and leather dressing with Mr Hepburn. There he found a wife and returned to ease the pressure of business on Thomas, whose success entailed civic leadership, especially after he added banking to the family interests. The bank was first Keep, Gotch & Cobb and finally Gotch & Sons, becoming the district's principal bank for three-quarters of a century.

The natural choice for chairing public meetings, Thomas presided at a momentous gathering at the White Hart (Royal Hotel) in 1803 when, with the nation facing invasion from France, Kettering people resolved to unite in defence of king and country and formed a corps of volunteers under the captaincy of John Cooper Gotch. War was the source of much of the Gotch wealth and influence, and when the peace of Amiens was announced Thomas was anxious for a good show of illuminations at Chesham House lest it should be said that as army contractors they regretted the peace. Candle lanterns were put in the trees by Jos Abrams with a long ladder, "making the best show in town — a very pleasing appearance".

With his son in the business, Thomas had less to do and was able to travel. In his chaise he went to spas and places of interest seeking relaxation and an improvement in health. His journeys took him to Wales, Buxton, Yarmouth, York, Liverpool, Chester and Shrewsbury, whence he wrote home describing and praising the towns and grumbling at the state of the roads until, in old age, he became the victim of a tiresome but unspecified malady which afflicted him with increasing weakness. He is always remembered for his recognition of the scholastic talent shown by William Carey, one of the shoemakers. Gotch left him free from the need to work so that he could study Latin and Hebrew, paying him a shilling a week more than he could have earned at his craft. Carey, Andrew Fuller and others met at Chesham House and the Mission House to form the Baptist Missionary Society, and Carey as the first missionary undertook immense pastoral work in India, translating and printing the Scriptures in native tongues.

John Cooper Gotch took over direction of the businesses when Thomas died in 1806. Born in the High Street house, he had succeeded his father at Chesham House on his marriage to Mary Ann Davis. His bride came from Chesham, where her father and grandfather were agents for the Dukes of Bedford, and as a second home to the Gotches her native town inspired the name of their Kettering residence. Mary Ann was descended on her mother's side from one of the signatories to the warrant for the execution of Charles I. Another ancestor was strong enough to survive an attack of the plague in 1665, and an odd fact handed down was that when as a girl her grandmother was ill all her hair was cut off and saved to make wigs for her father, perhaps in the belief that luxuriant hair consumed a patient's vital energies.

On the day the property and management of the leather, shoe and banking businesses devolved on John Cooper Gotch he wrote in his stockbook: "May I have the grace to improve whatever Providence may impart unto me, and while I lament the death of my much honoured parent, may I follow his steps in all that is praiseworthy and acceptable unto God." Though guided by a firm religious faith, he did not join Fuller Church until 1814, and his letters show that he was dismayed by the conditions laid down for membership. He agreed in due course, becoming auditor of the Baptist Missionary Society 1816-20 and serving on its committee 1830-43.

As the years passed, his social position in the town became as high as it could be. He was universally respected and beloved, and always ready to help and advise anyone who sought his aid. He was known for his wisdom, and was calm and vigorous, while his wife was benign and gracious. He took a leading part in all matters connected with the welfare of Kettering and, as captain of the Volunteers, was presented with a handsome sword by the NCOs and privates in recognition of his energy in organising their management and training.

He was leader of the Liberals in the northern part of the county, and through Lord Althorp had an effect on the Government of the day, particularly on questions affecting the Nonconformists. Many letters passed between Gotch and members of both Houses of Parliament, especially Earl Fitzwilliam, Lord Althorp and Lord Milton. In time it was chiefly as a banker that Gotch was known, and he became treasurer of a great number of societies and undertakings. Many of the Fitzwilliam letters indicate that the Earl freely placed at Gotch's disposal considerable sums in connection with the bank. At one time he lent £6,000 to tide over a difficult period, and Lord Sondes lent £10,000.

Gotch's importance as a key figure was shown in 1844 when Windsor Castle officials were in touch with him for advice about the intention that Queen Victoria and Prince Albert should call at Kettering on their way to Burghley House from Weedon, then the nearest railhead. In character were venison dinners at Chesham House for relations and friends. There were vast menus, but no alcoholic drinks, and the guests were all male. Those above the salt were fed rather better than those below. At the other extreme, he took a close interest in the poor as chairman of the Guardians for many years, and a new workhouse (now St Mary's Hospital) was built to the design of Sir George Gilbert Scott, whose major works were St Pancras and the Albert Memorial. The once-dominant central tower at St Mary's has been demolished.

With advancing age, John Cooper gradually yielded power and influence to his sons John Davis and Thomas Henry, making one his last public appearances in 1842 when he presided at the golden jubilee meetings of the Baptist Missionary Society. A guest for the two-day celebrations was his son-in-law, Thomas Hepburn of Clapham, who wrote a description for his wife, Mary Ann Gotch. He found the main tent, in the Mission House garden, filled with 5,000 people, and also packed were simultaneous meetings addressed by Mr Toller and Mr Robinson (ministers of Toller and Fuller), 1,500 attending one and 1,000 the other. Though Kettering's population was only 5,000, it entertained 7,000 visitors, and waiting carriages stood all the way from Lower Street to Market Place, where the Rector (Rev. Henry Corrie) opened the parish church for the day. Meetings were held in the streets, speakers moving from one to another with William Knibb, the courageous missionary and liberator of slaves, attracting the greatest following.

Hepburn found the lodging committee hard pressed. Hundreds could not get beds and the surrounding villages were full. At one place, 1,000 breakfasted together. He had to sleep on a sofa, but got a few hours of comfort when he moved into one of the warm beds after other guests rose to go to an early prayer meeting. He heard that at the prayer meeting Mr Stean preached for 2½ hours, and his sermon was not much liked as he ventured into areas of controversy.

On the whole it was a joyous occasion: "The house looked well, with everything new and beautiful. Your father took the chair and everyone was enthusiastic and happy. All are talking of the delightful and joyous meeting, and I have enjoyed it much. I admire most the very efficient and extensive arrangements made and carried out by your brothers John and Thomas." There was only one cloud in the sky: the youngest daughter Frances was a cripple and had to be carried to a point from which she could see the proceedings.

Ten years later John Cooper Gotch died. He had been a resourceful head for 46 years, and words from the oration at his funeral have survived, though not the name of the orator: "For the greater part of his life and to its end he was recognised as the leading man in the town which he adorned. A prominent actor in the storms of political life, and a welcome guest in the mansions of the great, he was rent in spirit though brightened in reputation by one the most fearful monetary crises this country has ever known. He had to wend his way through scenes and influences infinitely varied, and some very perilous. He was a good man. I never heard of a single scene in which he did not appear as a friend of man and a servant of God." Mercifully he was saved from any knowledge of a second crisis and the catastrophic failure of his bank five years later.

He was succeeded jointly by John Davis Gotch, who took charge of the boot manufacturing and leather businesses, and Thomas Henry Gotch, who ran the bank. The third son, the Rev. Frederick William Gotch, was advised by the Rev. Thomas Toller to enter the ministry and left Kettering when a young man to study at Trinity College, Dublin, as the English universities were closed to dissenters. He took his degrees and in 1845 became classical and mathematics tutor at Bristol Baptist College. As a learned Hebraist he was asked to help in revising the Old Testament, and this became the great work of his life. He edited the *Revised English Bible* to the end of the pentateuch (the first five books), and went on to edit the Old Testament for the beautiful and scholarly edition produced by the Religious Tract Society. He was examiner in Hebrew at London University, wrote articles for the *Encyclopaedia Britannica*, *Smith's Dictionary of the Bible*, and various publications besides composing the words of hymns. He strengthened links with the Hepburns, marrying Charlotte as his first wife.

Meanwhile at Kettering the family seemed to prosper. John Davis, remaining a bachelor, lived in Chesham House and continued the manufacturing business on the same lines as his father, employing many families of outworkers. Thomas Henry, who married Mary Ann Gale, lived in Jasmine House at the junction of old Tanners Lane and Lower Street, and four of his children were born there. About 1853 he moved into the Mission House, so that for the next four years the brothers lived opposite one another in two of the largest and most attractive houses in the town, seemingly unassailable as businessmen and bankers.

The crash came unexpectedly in 1857. It was a staggering blow to the Gotches and to the town. The bank, in premises opposite the Royal Hotel at the top of West Street, suspended payment, and many organisations and individuals must have felt that the end of their world had come. I have told the story fully in *Old Kettering and Its Defenders* and need not dwell on it here. The collapse dragged down the shoemaking firm, so that Chesham House, the factory, currier's shop, tanyard, stocks of material and the Mission House all had to be sacrificed to meet the claims of creditors.

During the bankruptcy proceedings it was shown that the Gotches had been misled by the Rev. Alan Macpherson, curate of Rothwell and a chaplain to the East India Company who travelled widely on the continent at the expense of the bank, dreaming up wild schemes which never paid off. As chief debtor he owed £25,000, equal to at least £3 million at today's values. The judge found no trace of fraudulent conduct by the Gotch family, though he questioned whether there was a degree of neglect of duties as bankers which might be considered as nearly equivalent to fraud. Creditors got 15s 6d in the pound, and later the family paid further sums, probably in full.

To me the saddest feature on a personal level was that Thomas Henry, who was responsible for the bank, was a highly talented mathematician who had been working on one of the most difficult publishing tasks imaginable — a volume entitled *Logarithmic and Trigonometric Tables to Seven Places of Decimals*. An amateur astronomer of no mean ability who used advanced mathematics for his calculations, he had found mistakes in the four volumes of log tables then existing and prepared his own volume. It ran to 300 pages of closely-printed figures with 11 columns to the page, and "contained the logarithms of the natural numbers from 1 to 100,000, and logarithmic sines, tangents, co-tangents and cosines to every ten seconds for the first five degrees and to every 30 seconds for the remainder of the quadrant." Was his mind on this when it should have been on the problems of the bank?

Dr Trestrail of Bristol, who wrote about the family, said that the toil involved in the mere correction of proofs was appalling, to say nothing of the original labour of the calculations. I can well imagine the dazed reaction of the hand compositors at Joseph Toller's printing works when they were presented with the copy to set. Tollers did the production for Simpkins, Marshall & Co. who published the book, but Gotch's modesty made him refuse to let the work bear his name, and it can be recognised only by the Toller imprint.

After the crash, Thomas Henry and his family closed the doors of the Mission House and fled from Kettering, unable to face the townspeople. They sought refuge with Thomas Hepburn and his wife who, as Christopher Gotch says, must have been little less than angels. They had 11 children of their own, yet hosted Thomas, his wife and their five youngsters through much of the five years of their exile.

John Davis, of much tougher fibre and with no wife and family as hostages to fortune, stayed on in Kettering. He moved to a smaller house, faced such setbacks as being dismissed by Fuller as its treasurer, obtained loans from the Hepburns, Gales and others to discharge the debts, rebuilt the business, and secured discharge from bankruptcy. A clue to his character was his demeanour when there was some election rowdyism on the market place and an officer in charge of yeomanry seemed about to fire into the crowd. "Give me that pistol," Gotch ordered, and was obeyed.

Says Christopher: "The sequel to the crash is a marvellous story. Kettering stood by the Gotches in their distress. Sterling friends were J. T. Stockburn who held Chesham House during their exile and sold it back on favourable terms, and a landowner named Hobson who helped with cash. In their letters John Davis is revealed as a stalwart, Thomas Henry as a wimp, and Frederick as little less than a monster. As the largest creditor he stood to suffer most, and the other two brothers hardly dared to make a move without consulting him. They suffered from such dreadful indecision that it is a wonder they recovered at all."

The affair led directly to the passing of the Limited Liability Act of 1858 which students of banking law are required to study. As the law stood then, even the legacies of Thomas Gotch and John Cooper Gotch were impounded.

Recovery was well on the way in 1861 when Thomas Henry wrote to J. T. Stockburn asking how Kettering would receive him and his family if they returned. JTS gave the green light, and the family came back in 1862, lived in Newland Street until 1871, then bought back Chesham House from Stockburn. They must have been light of heart when they crossed the threshold of their home once more.

The spin-off from the bank crash brought fresh opportunities for Kettering. On the break-up of the Gotch empire, young men who had learned shoemaking expertise as their employees became industrial leaders. The railway opened up distant markets and there seemed no limit to possible expansion. New firms were founded, and families moved in from the country knowing there would be plenty of jobs and a choice of houses for rent in the new streets. The population grew from 7,184 in 1871 to 19,454 in 1891, and by 1911 it was 29,972.

John Davis Gotch, the lonely bachelor who had restored the family's good name, died at 68 in 1870, his life's work done. Thomas Henry, back in the saddle, lived on at Chesham House surrounded by a fine young family — Henry Gale 23, Davis Frederick 21, John Alfred 19, Thomas Cooper 17, and Jessica 13. Rosa had died in 1858 aged seven. A hypochondriac, his health was his hobby and he kept going until 1891 when he died aged 87.

The four boys, all destined for eminence, went first to Mr Foy's academy in Chelsea and to Kettering Grammar School after the family returned. Henry, after whom Henry Gotch School is named, joined a school drum and fife band, played in a flute quartet, then graduated to the cello which remained his favourite instrument. He was for 24 years in the family shoemaking business at Kettering, went for a spell with a London publishing house, then in 1901 became secretary and a director of Mobbs & Lewis the lastmakers. His spare time interests were in music and education. He revived the Choral Society, conducted it, and played the cello in orchestral concerts. He became president of the Operatic Society on its foundation in 1919, and always contributed to speeches that followed the final curtain. Among several presentations to him was a gold watch from the Choral Society which was taken by a pickpocket on a London station. He bought a duplicate and had it re-inscribed with a reference to the theft of the previous one.

In education he held a record of useful work longer than many people's lifetimes. It began in 1869 when he became secretary to the management committee of the British School. He was the first chairman of the Education Committee 1903-6, serving on it until 1934 after being a member through the whole period of its existence. He was chairman of the governors of the old and new Grammar Schools, was 22 years a Guardian, 20 years a magistrate, served as chairman of the Urban Council 1906-7, and was a county alderman 1915-36. He married his cousin Mary Hepburn, also a Guardian and a member of the hospital board of management, and there were three sons and a daughter. They were both ill on their golden wedding day in 1939, and he was too unwell to attend the opening of the school named after him, dying a fortnight later aged 90. He was a Liberal, an Alpine climber, and an expert at chess.

Davis Frederick maintained links with the staple industries. He was first in the family shoe business, then spent eight years in partnership with William Timpson before becoming area representative for Hepburn & Gale. He was chairman of the School Board for the whole of its existence from 1890 until 1902, when it became the Local Education Authority. Under him it had a fine school building record — Stamford Road in 1892, Rockingham Road 1893, Hawthorn Road 1894-5, Park Road 1898-9 and Spencer Street (later the Central) 1902. Both his marriages formed links with families prominent in the staple industries. The first was to Maud Mursell, whose sister Katherine was the second wife of William Timpson, and the later one was to Ethel Hepburn whose sister Mary married Henry Gale. Maud and Katherine were two of nine orphan children of the Rev. James Mursell the younger, of Fuller, who died at 45 after leaving Kettering for Liverpool.

Davis's son Laurence Gotch became an architect, serving an apprenticeship with his uncle John Alfred at Gotch & Saunders, becoming an instructor at the Architectural Association's school of architecture, and going to Canada in 1910. He returned to serve as a captain in the Royal Engineers during the 1914-18 war and received the Order of the Nile for his work in the Middle Eastern campaign. After the war he returned to Kettering and he and his wife Auriel lived at Chesham House 1923-32. There were three children — Paul, Christopher and Anthea. He was junior partner in Gotch & Saunders, designing many banks, the first Kettering council estate to the east of Stamford Road, and advising on the Wicksteed Park pavilion and the *Evening Telegraph* office in Dryland Street, Burton Latimer manor house, the George Hotel, Kettering Cricket Club pavilion and other schemes. In 1930 he left the partnership to concentrate on bank work, designs for Stewarts & Lloyds, and the business of his London office. While in Kettering he was noted for his lectures on Lawrence of Arabia, whom he knew.

John Alfred Gotch was a little boy of five when his father's bank crashed. After he went to the Thomas Hepburns at Clapham Common he was so sensitive about what had happened that he hid letters he received expressing sympathy, and they were not found until Christopher started researching the family papers. JA was destined to be an eminent architect, but at first had no idea about a career. In his *Notes on the Family of Gotch* he recalls that in his younger days the family observed the strictest of Nonconformist Sundays, with even the mildest games ruled out. One suggestion was that he should enter the ministry, but his mother wanted him to be a lawyer.

From the Grammar School, he went to Zurich to complete his secondary education at the Polytechnic and the University. He returned to King's College, London, for one year and then to the Architectural Association for one year — the full course was seven years — before being articled with Charles Saunders to R. W. Johnson of Melton Mowbray who had a Kettering office. He went into partnership with Saunders and they built houses, schools, banks and war memorials in great numbers across the country. It was due in large measure to their inspiration and designs that Kettering became such a pleasant industrial town.

Gotch was an admirer of the old building crafts, and had no sympathy with contemporary trends. He was an authoritative writer on architectural subjects, and as an architectural historian has been hailed as the precursor of Pevsner and Summerson. His books include *Architecture of the Renaissance in England*, *The Growth of the English House*, *Inigo Jones*, *The Buildings of Sir Thomas Tresham*, *A Short Account of Haddon Hall*, *Kirby Hall*,

John Alfred Gotch was a little boy when the bank crashed. His family left Kettering for a while but later returned, and JA as a distinguished architect helped to restore the Gotch fortunes. In 1938 he was elected Charter Mayor. (Borough Council)

Holiday Journeys in Northamptonshire, and two county volumes dealing with squires' homes, old halls and manor houses. His renown as an architectural historian was acknowledged in 1923 when he was elected president of the Royal Institute of British Architects, the first provincial member to hold the office, president of the Architectural Association, and an honorary MA of Oxford University. He and his wife, Annie Perry, lost their son Roby Myddleton Gotch and their son-in-law Archibald Henry Pinxton Davey in the 1914-18 war, both killed in action.

In 1938 when Kettering became a borough he was accorded the highest honour the town could give, being appointed Charter Mayor with the responsibility of receiving the charter from the Lord Lieutenant, the Marquess of Exeter, and leading the borough celebrations. A great day was arranged. The charter was to be presented on the market place, with a concert of hymns and national songs by the schoolchildren, and with a civic luncheon to follow.

Things turned out very differently. Charter day came in the midst of the Munich crisis. The country was on the brink of war. Hitler was poised to invade Czecho-Slovakia, Chamberlain flew to intervene and, with Europe ready to explode, Chamberlain and Daladier met Hitler and Mussolini at Munich. The celebrations were cancelled. The charter was presented at a brief ceremony in the Regal Cinema (Granada), a short service followed, and I can still see in my mind's eye the subdued procession as, at the age of 86, J. A. Gotch wearing the mayor's scarlet robe led the company to the war memorial, so soon to bear the names of many more young townspeople. He laid a wreath "From the Borough of Kettering, in Remembrance." Chamberlain brought back the scrap of paper, but nobody was fooled. Plans to evacuate 11,000 London children to Kettering were merely postponed, the assembly and issue of gas masks and the establishment of first aid posts went ahead, and orders were issued that air raid shelter trenches must not be filled in. The rest is history. J. A. Gotch died in January 1942, ending the family's residential link with Kettering.

Thomas Cooper Gotch, youngest of the four talented brothers, spent three years with the family boot firm before studying art in Antwerp, at Heatherleys, at the Slade and in Paris. He went on a voyage to Australia, and then in London helped to form the Royal British Colonial Society of Artists and the New English Art Club. He married Caroline Yates, also an artist of distinction. They discovered Newlyn in 1879 and settled there in 1887. Bearded, hatless, and never needing glasses, he was an athletic figure with Alpine climbing as one of his interests.

His pictures, largely of children and subjects in the bloom of youth composed around a theme, attracted great attention, winning awards in Paris and Berlin, and through the years found places in the world's principal galleries. He was aided in his paintings by the beauty of his only daughter Phyllis, the model for some of his pictures and the inspiration of the child stories of H. D. Lowry. Titles of some of his famous pictures evoke their subjects — *Children and Maidenhood*, *Golden Youth*, *Holy Motherhood*, *A Pageant of Childhood*, *The Child Enthroned* and *A Golden Dream*. *The Message*, after being on loan to the Northampton Art Gallery for 40 years, was sold in 1990 for £150,000 to the Tainan Chi-Mai Arts Foundation, South Taiwan. He considered his best picture to be *Death the Bride*, which presented a less-forbidding view of death and set his work on a new course.

The Times thought him an artist who boldly struck out on an original line when realism was in fashion. Christopher Gotch feels that, as one of the Newlyn artists, TC achieved little renown, but after visiting Florence in 1891 he changed his style dramatically. From then on his work received considerable notice. Christopher concludes that his great-uncle holds a unique place in art history as a one-off not easily categorised, but certainly among the great Victorians and painters of the 20th century. He died in Brompton Hospital in 1935 aged 76. Phyllis became the Marquise de Verdieres and lived at Kettering for a

Thomas Cooper Gotch, whose works are in galleries worldwide, holds a unique place in art history, ranking both with the great Victorian painters and among moderns of the 20th Century. This was a self-portrait.

(Borough Council)

time, taking a great interest in artistic affairs.

Back now to John Gotch the butcher, mentioned at the start of this chapter. In 1828 John's grandson, John Speechley Gotch, was born. He was sent to school at Tollington Park, London, and apprenticed to a chemist at Market Harborough. After five years he emigrated and became a dentist's assistant in New York. In 1853 he sailed for Australia but was wrecked off Mauritius and earned his living as a dentist there before before going on to Melbourne. He tried gold digging but found nothing, so returned to Melbourne and sold newspapers for Alexander Gordon who had a market stall. They became partners as Gordon & Gotch, and by devoted work became Melbourne's main news and advertising agents and distributors of newspapers and magazines from Britain.

They opened branches in Sydney, Brisbane and London, added printing, publishing, advertising and the import of machinery to their activities, and when the London branch embarked on general exports such items as pianos and sewing machines were supplied throughout Australia. Gordon & Gotch went public in 1885 with John as chairman and later president, opening more branches. John's wife was Elizabeth Miller Jones from Bedford, and their sons were long associated with the firm, which became known across the world. The visit of Thomas Cooper and Carrie was at the invitation of John and Elizabeth with whom they stayed for three months in 1884. John bought TC's *Mental Arithmetic* and donated it to Melbourne City Art Gallery.

Christopher sums up the plus factors in the Gotch family's attainments: "Gotch, Hepburn, Gale and Berrill intermarried constantly. The families, Baptists and Quakers, could achieve power only through money and industry, hence intermarriage and nepotism, the secret of their success. Not until the mid-19th century could dissidents be local councillors, MPs or JPs, nor until 1871 attend any university. Despite this they were a political influence not to be dismissed for they were radical Liberals with no mean clout. After 1871, when the dissidents had achieved acceptance, their offspring entered the professions and made their mark."

Christopher was born in 1923. He spent five years as a fighter/bomber pilot in World War II, became an architect with his own firm in London, and for ten years was architectural critic of the *Hampstead and Highgate Express*, a local paper of considerable reputation. His books are *Corsica* (1952), *Art, Sex and Symbol* (1974), *A Privileged Education* (1978) and *The Grip of Freemasonry* (1991). He proposes to write a biography of T. C. Gotch.

His elder brother Paul married in 1938, and for their honeymoon he and his wife cycled through Europe as a pair of modern troubadours, but the journey ended in Athens when the Germans invaded Greece. In Egypt the British Council enrolled him for the next 45 years, posting him worldwide. He retired from a lifetime of exile in 1975 and was awarded the OBE.

A connection of 139 years with Chesham House ended in 1932 when Laurence Gotch and his family left for Hampstead. Among their interests, Mrs Auriel Gotch was superintendent of Cytringan Division of St John, and this was a farewell photograph.
Front row (left to right): Miss Madge Chapman, Miss Eva Bellamy, Miss Field. Middle row: Mrs Hales, Mrs Florence Ireson, Mrs Moore, Mrs Gotch, Mrs Vera Cross, Miss G. Luck, Miss Barnes. Back row: Miss N. Walden, Miss Kate Pell, Mrs Nunley, Mrs Sally Julian, Miss C. Franklin, Miss Ward and Miss Rose Walden. (*Audrey Sharman*)

THE STOCKBURNS

The record of the Stockburns in Kettering is both the story of a family and the life of a remarkable man, John Turner Stockburn, who was born under George IV, lived through the reigns of William IV, Victoria and Edward VII and was still hale and hearty and exercising personal power in the middle years of George V. He came of a line of innkeepers and local tradesmen who farmed as a sideline and passed on to him that ace in the game of life — an iron constitution. His father Joseph Stockburn lived to 90, and JTS, destined to reach 96, kept fit by hunting with the Pytchley, always well mounted and with a sound knowledge of the country.

When he was born in 1825 his father was running a drapery business on the corner of Market Street where Barclays Bank now stands. Joseph, who lived over the shop, was anxious to give his son a good grounding in life and sent him in turn to ten different schools, among them one at Cranford, Kettering Grammar School, and others at Market Harborough and Leicester. At Leicester his Liberal sympathies were strengthened through lodging with Edward Miall, an Independent minister, founder and editor of the weekly *Nonconformist*, and later MP for Rochdale and Bradford.

From school his father sent him on a four-year apprenticeship with a draper in Canterbury, an experience giving social insight that would be useful in political life later on. When he returned to Kettering his father was in partnership with John Goosey, and their drapery business occupied a house, shop and premises on the High Street site now covered by the Granada and its car park. In 1846, when JTS was 21, Joseph considered him skilled enough to need paternal guidance no longer and retired, leaving him in partnership with Goosey.

151

By now JTS had developed new ideas. Every woman who could afford them wore corsets as an aid to elegance, and he knew that manufacturing would be far more profitable than running a shop. He joined with his brother-in-law Robert Wallis, one of another Nonconformist family who had interests in milling, chicory, mustard and spice, and left the drapery business. The partners started corset manufacture, built the factory in Northall Street, and when Robert died Stockburn continued alone, achieving considerable prosperity. At 32 he was able to buy the Mission House which with its grounds formed an urban mini-estate. It was his home for 64 years and for a time he also owned Chesham House opposite, both acquired after the Gotch crash. He retired in 1887, leaving the business which included an extensive wholesale branch to his sons.

He attended Toller Church, and later its offshoot London Road Congregational Church, and was a leading county Liberal, securing the election of "Bobby" (later Lord) Spencer for North Northants in 1880, and after the rearrangement of seats introducing as candidate for the 1885 election Francis Channing who served as MP with striking success for a quarter of a century. JTS himself took a hand on the Parliamentary scene, challenging Lord Burghley in North Northants in 1892 and losing by only 669 votes — 4,505 to 3,836.

JTS did as much as anyone to make Kettering a better place in which to live. In the mid-1800s the domestic water supply came from shallow wells, all more or less polluted. He tried to persuade the Vestry, which then ran public affairs, to establish a mains supply for the town. Getting no response, he led the way in establishing Kettering Water Co., becoming its chairman. The company built a pumping station and reservoir producing a pure supply, and eventually Kettering Urban Council acquired the system by compulsory purchase.

He pressed for the adoption of the Local Government Act to establish the Local Board which in 1872 took over town administration from the Vestry. Stockburn became its chairman, was voted back into office when the Board became the Urban Council in 1894, and remained chairman until 1898 when, despite pressure to continue, he retired because of age — he was 73.

It was largely due to him that the School Board was established in 1890 after being many times outvoted on the grounds of expense. Other activities in a full life were opening up the Alexandra Street area for housing, membership of the County Council, many years chairmanship of Kettering Gas Co. and of Northamptonshire Printing & Publishing Co., owners of the *Evening Telegraph*. He presided at directors' meetings when in his 90s with as much lucidity and grasp of finances as ever. He led the way in establishing the General Hospital and in founding the Liberal Club, to which he gave its library. No wonder he was ''Mr Kettering'', always regarded as speaking for the town.

He had a stroke while walking in London Road, and was confined to bed in the Mission House for 17 months before he died aged 96, disabled but still mentally active. After his death the family traditions were carried on for many years by his youngest child, Miss Christine Stockburn, born in 1878, who reached her 100th year. She wanted a career in days when there were few openings for women, and chose art, working for a firm in London and studying at the National Gallery and the Victoria and Albert Museum, but in 1900 had to return home for health reasons. She then became more and more involved in a busy family life at the Mission House which was the focus of many town activities and a base for important political and religious guests of JTS. Before long her mother (née Eliza Osborn Smith) fell ill, and Christine had to take over full responsibility.

The atmosphere of the Mission House during the Stockburn years has been captured in her memoirs, which she wrote in an exercise book when over 80 as a 13th birthday present for her great-great-nephew David Squire, great-grandson of Harry Osborn Stockburn who was the third child of JTS and Eliza. David, a chartered accountant and a partner in Price Waterhouse, has kindly sent me a copy of the memoirs which are illustrated with many family photographs, and what follows is a condensed version which I hope retains all the richness of Christine's observations.

From her earlier years she was sent to visit people whom her parents befriended in days of great poverty for many families. For 30 years even the Stockburns' tea leaves were saved and on six mornings a week were collected with a milk pudding for a woman who was bedridden and nursed by two friends. Each Tuesday morning an old woman went past on her way to the butcher's for a halfpennyworth of liver, her meat for the week.

John Turner Stockburn in 1920 when aged 94, with his fellow directors
of the Evening telegraph who had a remarkable record of longevity and
service. Seated, left to right, are: Andrew Mackay, director 1916-43,
died 1943 aged 87; B. Jinks, director 1904-24, died 1924 aged 88; J.
T. Stockburn, director 1887-1922, chairman 1899-1922, died 1922 aged
96; Thomas Bird, director 1889-1927, chairman 1922-27, died 1927 aged
86; W. W. James, director 1887-95 and 1919-28, died 1929 aged 89.
Standing, left to right, are: A. G. Jones, director 1899-1924, died 1924
aged 66; J. A. Gotch, director 1895-1942, chairman 1927-42, died 1942
aged 89; Sir Richard Winfrey, MP, managing director 1901-44, died 1944
aged 85; Richard Winship Stockburn, director 1900-03, secretary
1901-24, son of J.T. Stockburn, died 1924 aged 62. (Jane Campbell)

Another earned her living by going from door to door with
a wooden yoke on her shoulders and a pail of milk on each side,
selling half-pints.

Dorcas meetings at the chapels made clothes to give away at
Christmas, and the Stockburn children spent autumn evenings
making unbleached calico underclothes and flannel petticoats
for poor people. A new sheet was one of the most prized gifts.
Each November and February, Mrs Stockburn sent two hundred-
weights of coal to old people requiring help.

J. T. Stockburn had a list of needy folk, and every Christmas
sent 4s to each married couple and 2s 6d to each single person.
There were so many that distributing the money and reporting
to their father on the situation of each person took the family
three weeks. Mrs Stockburn organised a Christmas party for all
the beneficiaries in the Mission Hall at the top of Tanners Lane.
One of them, Thomas Spence, had a wife crippled with arthritis

whom he waited on night and day, carrying her downstairs before he left for work. Feeling unwell, he went to Dr Price, who told him, "Tom, it's a holiday you want." On his next visit Tom said, "I've had that holiday, doctor." The doctor, surprised, asked where he had been, and was even more amazed when the old fellow replied: "To Mrs Stockburn's tea party."

Christine describes pay-day in Northall Street: "Friday afternoon was the time when all were paid at our corset factory, which we could reach through our garden. As each one came to the pay window, Father would inquire after his or her family, and they might ask for his help, perhaps with a letter of recommendation for Northampton Infirmary, then the nearest hospital.

"A singular collection of men and women worked there, and today we should think them pitifully poor. Mehetabel Chapman, head of the women's room, for example, earned 13s 6d a week. They all knew Mother, and were most interested when as a baby I was taken to see them. Mother was the most generous of women and spared no time or trouble, always giving of her best. Sometimes her gifts seemed such trifles, but looking back one realises how much they meant to those she helped. Eighty years later one old lady who had been a girl at the factory remembered taking a blancmange for her father who was dying, and tasting it on the way.

"On Saturday afternoons, Mother often took us to see her old laundress Mrs Biggs, and one day stopped at Chettle's shop on the market place to buy some oranges to take to the workhouse. She chose the best, but the assistant suggested that cheaper ones would do for the workhouse. He received a cutting reply: 'Young man, if you did not often have an orange, wouldn't you like the best when you did get one?' "

Mr Hudson looked after the furnace at the factory. He was short and stout, and used to fascinate the children by standing on the back of a tortoise he kept in the basement, and showing off passion flowers he had grown by the hot pipes. The tortoise came to a sudden end when it crawled into the furnace and was roasted.

JTS when appointed a magistrate in 1882 was one of the first two who were not from county families. He had always supported the Salvation Army, lending them the Mission House field for a meeting every Whit Monday, and it was no pleasure for him when the first case to come before him was a complaint against the Army for obstructing the roadway. Christine remembered the first bicycle she saw, and the first road accident. In her pram, with one wheel in front and two behind, she was being taken down The Piece (London Road) and was near the old brickyard when a cyclist came flying down the hill on a penny-farthing. The front wheel struck a rut, and he nose-dived over the handlebars. The children were impressed when they met the Rev. Thomas Toller, noted preacher, minister of Toller Chapel, and father of a large family of sons and daughters. The Piece was the route for his daily constitutional.

The Mission House cats, a necessity in an old building, were characters. Jebb and Mann were opposite in looks and nature but were devoted companions and always slept with paws around each others' necks. Their successors were Spy and Tenfil. Tenfil got shut in a box for nearly a week but was none the worse. Bill, who came later never lapped his milk but dipped his left paw and sucked it. He was not pleased if no cream was added. "Besides the cats there were endless pet animals — dogs galore, a fox, a magpie and horses. I loved them all so much that my clothes smelled of them and had to be shut out of the nursery window to air."

Home life at the Mission House ran smoothly and happily. Christine and her brothers and sisters grew up with few excitements, but they were taught to feel responsible for those who served the family, and for those in less comfortable circumstances. JTS read a chapter of the Bible each morning, and during the day the children were kept in the nursery, taken downstairs by the nursemaid only for meals and for a couple of hours after tea. If Mrs Stockburn wanted them down to see a visitor she rang a bell outside the dining room door, and the excursion would last about five minutes. Nursemaid Jane Marchant lived with the family all her active life, and often stayed as a friend after she retired.

Christine began lessons at home in 1883 when she was five, first from Mrs Annie Mansell and then Miss Miller. As soon as she could read a little she was sent on Sunday afternoons to read a chapter from the Bible to old Mrs Townsend: "Mercifully for her she was very deaf, and as I read only the smaller words, and spelt the long ones I did not know it was not very interesting for the poor old lady, but it was excellent training for me. We lived in a strong Nonconformist and political atmosphere, and I went to my first political meeting at Desborough when seven. Sir James Carmichael, private secretary to Mr Gladstone, was contesting North Northamptonshire and stayed with us when in the constituency. Sent to tell him tea was ready, I asked him to ask Mother to let me go with him and Father to the meeting. He said: 'What will you give me if I do?' I promptly said 'I will kiss you' — and did. Mother let me go, but I had to come home early by fly in charge of Mr Charles Pollard.''

She had no childhood friends. Her brother John went off to a boarding school at Leicester, and Miss Hurst, a governess, had charge of Christine and her elder sister Grace until in 1888 Grace went to Miss Mann's near the Zoo in London for finishing lessons. Christine was then placed in charge of Miss Earl, a young Irish governess. Mrs Stockburn's mother joined the household in her old age, and Miss Gray, a trained nurse, was engaged to look after her: "She wore a green uniform of cloak and bonnet, one of the first seen in Kettering. People used to turn to look at her in the street.''

Christine was taken to visit Miss Mann, one of whose neighbours lent her carriage so that the children could go to Hyde Park in the hope that Queen Victoria might go for a drive as she generally did after a Drawing Room: "Sure enough, I saw the little old lady — the only time in my life.''

In 1889 she was sent to Miss Lockett's boarding school at Hampstead, run by four sisters, where she stayed for four years. It was the first time she had been away on her own; she was homesick, found the strict rules irksome, and felt like a hen in a coop. There were 30 boarders and 100 day girls, including two daughters of Sir Alfred East. In later life, one of the girls married Lord Dawson of Penn, physician to George V. Pupils had to speak French for part of every day, which at first silenced Christine as she did not know a single word of the language.

To complete her schooling she moved to Miss Turner's in College Villas Road, chosen so that she could attend Lyndhurst Road Chapel where she heard many famous preachers. In 1895 she went for the first time to a theatre — the Lyceum — where she saw Ellen Terry in *The Merchant of Venice*. She visited the

Royal Opera House to see *Cavalleria Rusticana*, and Sir Augustus Harris gave the girls the Prince of Wales' box as his daughter received dancing lessons at Miss Turner's. "We were very conscious of people looking at us and wondering who we were. I'd had my hair dressed, and it cost 1s 6d."

When in 1900 she had to come home she was far from well, with slight curvature of the spine and an abscess under her right arm. She went to Suffolk to help her brother Harry and his wife Clare with their children, then came back to help Mr and Mrs Henry Gotch whose governess had left. She had charge of Rosa Gotch and Grace Wallis, who were seven, and Arthur Gotch and Ralph Wallis, both five, taking them for an hour's walk each afternoon.

By 1905 her mother (d. 1909) was in failing health and needed all the help that Christine could give. She took charge at the Mission House — a challenge greeted by JTS with the comment, "Now we'll see what you're made of."

In fact she coped so well that in time she gradually found leisure for other interests. She took up lace-making, was co-opted as a Liberal member of the Education Committee, and in response to an appeal from the Rev. W. L. Lee started a Sunday School class at London Road Church which grew to nearly 50 girls aged over 18. Christine noted: "This is the experience I most value in my life. It brought me friendships, not only of my girls but of their parents and their children and grandchildren. There is no more rewarding work than a Sunday School class with all its joys and anxieties." The girls were devoted to her, and when one was asked the reason she said, "She never asks questions." This was true — Christine had a rule always to wait to be told people's joys and sorrows.

She could be formidable. Once she was asked to take a class of disorderly boys which, unknown to her, had degenerated into a bear-garden, and obtained perfect order after the word went round, "Look out, it's Miss Stockburn." She found afterwards that the week before they had led a man teacher such a dance that he bolted and refused ever to take them again.

During the Stockburn years at the Mission House, many well-known political and free church figures stayed there, among them General Booth. On his tour by motor-car in 1907, he spoke at the Victoria Hall and went for tea before travelling on.

*Miss Christine Stockburn in 1928.
The youngest child of J. T. Stockburn, she ran
the Mission House as a family home and then
made charitable work her life interest,
donating the Stockburn Memorial Home as a
nurses' headquarters in memory of her
parents. She lived to her 100th year.
(David Squire)*

Christine describes the visit: "The previous week I received a printed list of what he would like — China tea made with boiled milk, mushrooms fried in butter, etc. At three o'clock his secretary arrived and explained that he would cook the General's tea. I refused to allow him in my kitchen, but let him interview my cook. At tea the General's staff stood until I made them sit down with us. He sat with his head in his hands, evidently tired, until Father told him that he had heard his wife, Catherine Booth, preach at the opening of the Kettering Citadel. Then he brightened up and talked at great length. Father said it was one of the best sermons he had ever heard."

JTS after his stroke in September 1920 never left his bed again, dying on February 2, 1922. The Rev. Charles Deeble, minister of London Road Church, said that in all his years there he had never seen the church so full as for the funeral, with all denominations represented. John Turner Stockburn had been a man they all trusted.

Under his will, the Mission House and his possessions had to be sold so that there could be an equitable division among the children. This meant that Christine had to move out of her lifelong home, even having the cat Bill put to sleep. More family deaths followed. She and her brother Dick went to lodge with Mrs Patrick in Kettering Road, Geddington, before buying No. 100 Roundhill Road. After a long illness, Dick died in 1924, and Christine moved to 8 Headlands, which people remember as her home for 50 years. She was joined there by brother John. In 1926 her brother Harry died at Bedford, followed two days later by his daughter Helen. They were buried at Kettering. The following year John died. Her sister Mary returned to Kettering first staying as a paying guest at the old home, now called Carey Guest House, then falling ill and being looked after by Christine. She passed on at Christmas 1927. They were sad years.

Left fairly free now, Christine travelled, sometimes with Grace and her husband, Percy Grundy. In Kettering she continued to devote herself to good causes besides resuming attendance at university lectures, having a companion-help at Headlands. She was elected a Guardian, and took the work very much to heart, showing a great interest in the problems of tramps and other unfortunates in the Institution. Once while she was with an official party carrying out an inspection, a little girl in the children's ward sidled up to her and said: "Please would you nurse me just a minute?" Christine sat down, took the child on to her knee, and stayed with her, leaving the rest of the party to finish the inspection.

One case was typical of the times. "The phone rang, asking me to go to see a girl who had come in the night before with her husband. They were tramps. Her family had objected to her marriage, and she was expecting a baby in a few months. The doctor said she must have a few days' rest, but her husband refused to do the work required of him, and I was asked to have a talk with her. Her people were in a good position, and her husband had brought her down to tramping from one workhouse to another. She would not let me write to her mother, and when I asked what she was going to do when her baby came, she said, 'Turn into the first workhouse I come to.' I often wonder what became of her."

In February 1928 she bought Belle Vue, the big house off Broadway, for use as accommodation for the district nurses and gave it to Kettering as the Stockburn Memorial Home, a striking act of generosity to commemorate her father and mother.

She always carved at the Infirmary dinner on Christmas Day. One patient was an orphan boy who was dying. She asked if there was anything he would like. He requested a Christmas annual which Christine obtained, and then said he would like to eat a rabbit's head and peas — the greatest delicacy he knew. The master of the institution promised to get him the meal but added: "You know, Miss Stockburn, he cannot eat anything and will not be here many days." The boy died, with the annual his only possession.

She was one of the Guardians appointed to visit the county asylum at Berrywood, and remembered many patients pleading to be allowed to come home. The visitors wrote down the names and promised to ask the doctor, doing their best to give reassurance. The most seriously ill were in padded cells and had to be observed through slits in the doors.

She was keenly interested in the infirmary as there were so many opportunities for service. Some patients had no friends, so she offered to get things they liked, write letters, lend a book or go on errands. Another side of her work was at London Road Church as president of the Northamptonshire Congregational Union, and a prime mover in forming the Northamptonshire Federation of Congregational Women. She visited all the Congregational women's meetings in the county, and became well known as a speaker.

Among her hobbies painting came first, but was limited after an accident left her right hand feeble. Next came reading, and then needlework. She took up making laces to Irish designs, first Carrickmacross and Limerick, then passed on to embroidery, making pulpit falls and communion cloths for churches. This was a family talent, shown when she exhibited in the Library a case of needlework done by her great-grandmother, grandmother, mother, and herself: "Men were equally interested, and many asked me about it."

Brothers who figure in her memories are Joseph, the eldest (d. 1905), father of her nephew Cyril who emigrated to Canada; Harry, who went with his wife Clare to New Zealand for a while and then settled in Bedford; Dick, who served as secretary of the Northamptonshire Printing & Publishing Co.; and John, who learnt estate management as a pupil on Lord Rosebery's estate. Her sisters were Mary, who made a career in nursing, and Grace who became Mrs Percy Grundy. Her nephew Cyril farmed in Canada, served in France with the 230 Battalion in the 1914-18 war, then worked for the Canadian Pacific Railway 1925-42, retiring to Winnipeg. He left three sons, two daughters and 18 grandchildren. Harry's daughter Phyllis came to stay with Christine at the Mission House to attend Kettering High School, as did Katherine Linnell, a second cousin from Desborough.

Others she recalls include Mrs Gunton, her companion-help at Headlands for 18 years whose capability left her free for work in the town; Raymond Ralph, gardener at Mission House; Gussie Gascoyne, her cousin; and Gertie Barber, a lifelong friend from schooldays whose father was a Sheffield doctor. Nursemaid Jane Marchant's three brothers were tailors at Stanwick and made all JTS's clothes for over 70 years.

I was delighted with a story dating from 1881 when Christine was aged three. A large family party led by JTS, who resembled the Prince of Wales, later Edward VII, went on holiday to Hunstanton. The royal railway carriage was being returned to Sandringham via Kettering, and the stationmaster offered the Stockburns the use of it: "I have been told, though I have no recollection of it, that the upholstery was blue satin. We caused some excitement when the train stopped at Cambridge, my sister Mary and Gussie Gascoyne putting baskets reversed on their heads. People on the platform gazed in, thinking them to be strangely attired foreigners travelling with the Prince and Princess of Wales."

As one of the Guardians responsible, Christine recalled the occasion in the 1920s when Kettering received honourable mention in *Punch* because of the high reputation the Public Assistance Institution had for the treatment of all under its care, particularly the tramps who spent the night there, 6,661 passing through in the course of a year. Following national publicity about this, *Punch* made the following comment:

> The casual wards of England
> > Are various in cheer;
> Some are benevolently run,
> > Others are more severe;
> But Kettering, oh! Kettering
> The home from home of Kettering
> Is good beyond all bettering
> > And stands without a peer.
>
> The vagabonds of England,
> > Barring when cold or damp,
> Prefer the skies for canopy
> > And the pale moon for lamp;
> But Kettering, ah! Kettering,
> The evening bell of Kettering
> Will never fail to get a ring
> > From any neighbouring tramp.

The householders of England
    Are liberal to the core,
They like to pay the union rate
    And wish that it were more;
But Kettering, my Kettering,
I claim the palm for Kettering
Which carves in golden lettering
"Welcome" above its door.

From David comes the story of J. T. Stockburn's steadfast courtship of Eliza. Her father, John Winship Smith, was a surgeon who came of a Kettering family. He married Charlotte Ellen Marshall, and practised at Woodbridge, Suffolk, in partnership with his brother-in-law, but died when still young. With her mother Eliza returned to Kettering, and JTS saw her out walking when she was only 12 and still in black mourning. It was love at first sight. They were married after a long friendship when she was 18 and her bridegroom 23.

THE BARLOWS

When 86, Mrs Doris Butlin compiled from memory a 6,000-word account of the Barlow family, full of human interest. She gave me the manuscript, and I have based this shorter version on it. Head of the family when she was young was her great-great-uncle Edward Barlow. He had eight sons, four daughters and 42 grandchildren, with many great-grandchildren, so that well over 50 family members and relatives by marriage figure in the story. Doris had a further link with the family by her marriage to Norman Butlin, one of Edward Barlow's grandsons. She was daughter of Harry Mobbs, one of the founders of Mobbs & Lewis, later Mobbs Miller, and reached her hundredth birthday on January 31, 1992.

Edward Barlow (1829-91) was a builder and brickmaker during the years of Kettering's great expansion. He lived in Rothwell, and had brickworks there and in Kettering on land now built over between Wellington and Tresham Streets. In 1869 he was the contractor for St Andrew's Church, for which the architect was George Edmund Street (1824-81), famous for his parish churches. Street restored York Minster and Salisbury Cathedral, designed the Crimea memorial church at Istanbul, and crowned his career with the Law Courts in the Strand. He is buried in Westminster Abbey.

In the 1880s Edward built the famous Old Post Office block in Gold Street, destroyed in 1976 to make way for Newlands, and he erected one of the first Headlands houses, Lonsdale, called "the castle" because originally it had a tower, turret and crenellated walls. Costing £1,000, Lonsdale was built for Doris's great-uncle, shoe manufacturer William Hanger (1828-90). He came of an old Kettering weaving family and when weaving declined he started shoemaking in the former weaving mill in

School Lane. Most shoe manufacturers were Nonconformists and Liberals, but William was Church of England, and his nephew Henry widened the gulf by standing for the Local Board as a Tory. Henry succeeded to the business and built the factory on the Stamford Road-Wellington Street corner.

While Lonsdale was being built Headlands was still a private country lane, and when Teddy Barlow — as everyone knew him — went by horse and trap to inspect the work his daughter Ada had to get down at the Bowling Green Road corner to open the gate. Doris describes Teddy as a right good fellow with a ready wit, fond of convivial evenings which often left him too far gone to drive home. In those days that was no problem. Horses could, and often did, find their own way home with the reins hooked round the fingers of an unconscious reveller in the driver's seat.

Teddy used to tell against himself the story of one such excursion. Fast asleep in his dog cart he was returning from Kettering to Rothwell, but the horse went off the road and got the vehicle stuck. A passer-by with a sense of humour unhitched the horse which went home by itself, leaving Teddy to slumber on. He was astounded when he woke in the morning under the open sky, with no horse and green fields all around. "I couldn't think where I was, or whether I'd lost a horse or found a cart," was the way he summed up the adventure. Similar tales have been handed down about other people.

In her story Doris lists the 12 children presented to Teddy by his wife, Elizabeth Slow — Edwin, Fred, Charles, Henry, Alfred, Edward Arthur, Ada, Martha (Pat), Luther, Polly, Fan and Evan — and then relates anecdotes about them and their families.

Edwin Barlow, the eldest, was unlucky. Like his father he became a builder, specialising in work on churches, but his career was ruined when he fell from a church tower he was repairing. He survived, but severe concussion handicapped him permanently and he was never so successful as his brothers.

Fred, the second son, was a leading figure in Rothwell. A builder, he also farmed at Thorpe Underwood, developed an interest in agricultural machinery, and acquired the old-established agricultural implement business of Ball & Son. The foundry and works were behind a high brick wall, and the S-bend near the church shows where the A6 rounded the site. The office entrance opposite Fox Street was distinguished by a model

of the firm's prizewinning horse-drawn plough which orna-
mented the portico, and a story I heard from a 90-years-old
Rowellian but cannot vouch for was that the business changed
hands as the result of a wager between the two families. Housing
now occupies the ground.

Fred Barlow showed ability early in life. At 17 he was elected
to the committee of the British School, and by 21 he was
secretary and manager of Rothwell Gas Company. In local
politics he served 22 years as chairman of the local Board/Urban
Council, and under him the water and sewage systems were
constructed, the gasworks was acquired by the town, the
swimming bath was opened, council offices and public library
were completed, roads were widened and trees planted. He was
Rothwell's county councillor, a Guardian, a JP, first officer of
the St John Ambulance, helped to establish the Volunteers, and
conducted the Wesleyan choir.

The council offices and library were built into the Market
House when at Fred's suggestion it was completed to mark
Queen Victoria's golden jubilee. The building, a neighbourly
gift to the town from Sir Thomas Tresham of Rushton Hall, was
left unfinished after the Treshams were ruined by the Gun-
powder Plot, and had stood a roofless shell for 300 years. Fred,
with pardonable pride in his achievement, had his initials FB
carved on a blank shield among the arms of County families
which form a frieze round the building, but in recent years some
purist has had them rubbed off. A pity. They were part of history,
and for me that was the shield with a human story.

Fred, in the same style, constructed the Jubilee Spring in
Kettering Road, much in demand in horse transport days, and
brought white marble from Italy when he visited the Carrara
quarries to build the front steps of the White House, adapted from
an older building as his residence.

He was beaten in an election only once, in 1900 when he stood
for Parliament against Col. Stopford Sackville. Fred had toured
the constituency making rousing Liberal speeches but took his
defeat withour rancour. "I was well whacked," was his
comment. Like many of the Barlows he suffered from heart
trouble, and was forced to limit his business activities for some
years before dying at 61 in 1916. His wife was Sarah Ann
Whymant of Clipston.

Fred and Sarah had a family of two sons and four daughters. Ernest died young, and Lancelot went to Howards of Bedford to qualify as an agricultural engineer, returning to take charge of Ball & Son. He married Elsie Butlin, they lived at the White House, and their son David became head of the music department at Newcastle College, Durham University. A composer, he wrote a symphony based on resonant cadences remembered from John Wood's Latin lessons at Kettering Grammar School. It was broadcast by the BBC, and one of his choral works was commissioned by the Rev. Walter Hussey of St Matthew's, Northampton. David died in early middle age, also from heart trouble.

Fred gave his elder daughters a beautiful double wedding. Mabel married George Ward Sumner of Desborough who farmed and trained hunters and polo ponies at a riding school in the Buckwell Street area, now built over. The Sumners had been farmers and leading residents for over 200 years, and George did a long spell as council chairman. Eve married Will Pacey of Pacey's Ales, Melton Mowbray, who was then gaining experience in a Kettering bank. Doris Butlin says: "The girls decided on a double wedding because they were very much kindred spirits. It was a splendid affair, most of the girl cousins acting as bridesmaids, clad in many pastel shades of silk and providing a lovely entourage.

"At the reception the brides sang favourite duets, their voices blending harmoniously to the great enjoyment of the guests."

They were both to die early. The influenza epidemic of 1919 was responsible for Mabel's death. She left three small children, George, Dick and Margaret. In the last war, George, a captain in the Leicestershire Regiment, served in Burma with General Wingate's force behind the enemy lines. Dick, a warrant officer in the RAF, was injured at Dunkirk, served as an instructor in Canada, and came home for D-Day. He died in hospital in 1945 after an operation. Margaret married Richard Biggins, manager of the Desborough ore processing works, and eventually the links with Desborough were severed.

Eve was the victim of a road accident. She and Will Pacey lived at Melton Mowbray where he went into his father's business. Frances and Billy were the children, and Billy became a Bentley enthusiast who raced at Brooklands. In summer 1930, the family were holidaying at West Runton and Billy was driving his mother down to join them. Just as a welcome was being prepared, news came that the car had been in a crash, and Eve had been thrown out and killed.

Fred's younger daughters were Ella and Margery. Ella married her cousin Edward Butlin, Norman's brother. He was a schoolmaster at Harrow, then became in turn headmaster of new mixed educational schools at Finchley and Harrow Weald. He retired to Orlingbury after Ella died. Margery was Doris's special friend at Kettering High School, and they often caught Arch's horse bus from High Street to Rothwell, joining other school friends for parties at the White House. Margery married Horace Wright, familiarly known as Hob, later head of George Wright Ltd, Kettering shoe manufacturers. Hob, Lance and Norman were all early motorbike owners, and Doris was deafened by repeated engine tuning.

Teddy's third son, Charles Barlow, was to Burton Latimer what

Charles Barlow (1857-1923) and his wife Deborah. Charles started as a grocer's apprentice and soon owned three shops — grocer, draper and butcher — at the midpoint of Burton Latimer High Street. He farmed, figured in local government, and mined limestone and iron ore, transported in a fleet of railway wagons bearing his name. His wife was niece of Ann Sharpe who ran a school for young ladies at Harrowden Hall, and taught and later sheltered crown princess Kaiulani of Hawaii. (Douglas Ashby)

169

his brother Fred was to Rothwell. After completing his apprenticeship to a grocer, he established himself as a businessman and farmer. His grocers, drapers and butchers shops were all at the central point of Burton High Street, and he gradually acquired farms nearby and at Faxton and Scaldwell. Some of the land lay above limestone and ironstone which Charles quarried and supplied to ironworks all over the country in a fleet of railway wagons bearing his name.

He married Deborah Maria Sharpe, and they lived at The Yews, Kettering Road, which Deborah inherited from he aunt, Mrs Ann Sharpe. Douglas Ashby recalls that The Yews had a history which attracted many visitors who knew of its connection with Hawaii. For centuries until Captain Cook discovered them in 1778, the Hawaiian Islands had lain at peace. The handsone natives, who managed to live without pottery, metals or beasts of burden, were unequalled as sailors, navigators and swimmers. The power to rule descended through both male and female members of their royal family.

Though killed by the natives in the following year, Cook had opened the islands to western influences. At first the people were pro-British, despite a tragedy in 1824 when the king and queen visited England and both died in a measles epidemic. Links with the United States gradually developed; in 1893 a provisional government favouring union with the US came to power, and the last royal ruler, Queen Liliuokalani, was deposed with no hope of restoration.

Liliuokalani had sent the beautiful Princess Kaiulani, the last crown princess of Hawaii, to England for her education and so that she could live in safety. She was placed with Mrs Sharpe, who was proprietress of an exclusive school for young ladies of rank at Harrowden Hall, and on completing her education the princess went to live as an exile in Jersey. When it became evident that she could never go home to Hawaii, she turned in her distress to her old schoolmistress. Ann Sharpe had retired to The Yews, and gladly made her welcome there, but the princess lived only a few more years and died at 23. Researchers who came in 1970 to write her story felt that, heartbroken, she had lost the will to live.

The Yews passed to Deborah and Charles after Ann died in 1898. They had a family of six — Frank, Alfred, Lily, Harold,

Arthur and Daisy — and Doris Butlin paid many visits to the house, which had big gardens, an orchard and a tennis court: "I often went with cousins to spend a happy day, robbing the orchard and riding our bikes home with as much fruit as we could carry tucked into our elastic-hemmed blouses."

The impact of the Barlows on local affairs is shown by the roles they filled simultaneously. Charles was chairman of the Board of Guardians and vice-chairman of Kettering Rural Council; his younger brother Henry was chairman of Kettering Urban Council; and his elder brother Fred was chairman of Rothwell Urban Council. His sons Frank and Arthur were members of Burton parish council. Family mementoes are an inscribed manuscript illustrated with Burton Latimer scenes painted by J. A. Gotch and presented in gratitude for Charles's public work, a framed tribute from his friend Charles Wicksteed, and the silver key he used to open the Warkton Lane reservoir building, which descended respectively to grandsons Roland, Ivan and John.

Henry Barlow, Teddy's fourth son, struck out on a new line as a baker and confectioner. The bakery was in Stamford Road, and the delightful Mikado Cafe in Newland Street became a favourite meeting-place, its first-floor bow window a gazebo overlooking the Gold Street crossroads. The Japanese decor and furnishings were a novelty in the inter-war years. Henry farmed off Rothwell Road, and bred horses with prizewinners among them. His son Gladstone expanded the business and opened three more shops, maintaining the equine interest by breeding hunters and riding to hounds. Henry had three daughters, Maud, Winifred and Phyllis.

Doris recalls Teddy's fifth son, Alfred, as a builder with the General Hospital, Rockingham Road and Stamford Road Schools, and many private houses to his credit. His wife was Ella Mobbs, Doris's aunt, and they lived first in Carrington Street and then at Enderslie, a fine old house in Mill Road with a big garden, orchard and stables. When factories were built and the street changed its character the family moved to The Drive, then a new area. Alfred erected seven houses, three facing Headlands, and intended to build one for himself on the corner, but before he could do so he fell ill and was advised to take a Mediterranean cruise. He was no better when he returned and, despite specialist advice, died so suddenly that there was no time to call his doctor.

He was only 39, but left £30,000, worth millions at today's values. The site of the house he had planned remained vacant for years, but the garden flourished and formed a paradise in which Doris and her cousins played.

Alfred and Ella had three daughters, Margaret, Nesta and Edna. Bedford was then the nearest high school, but Ella did not wish the girls to commute by train or to become boarders. She moved to Bedford and lived there until their schooling finished. Nesta married Kenneth Bryson, son of a noted scholar and missionary to China, who worked for a firm of merchants and was stationed at Tientsin. She went out for the wedding, taking her most-treasured possession — her grand piano. They had hardly settled in their new home when Kenneth received orders to move to Chungking, a thousand miles up the Yangtse. This proved an exciting journey, as the boat had to be hauled up rapids by a gang of 500 coolies, urged on by shouts and the cracking of whips. Doris adds:

"I used to hear from Nesta every week when I was at school in Switzerland. The tales she told were entrancing. House-keeping wasn't easy for a young bride, as many items had to be ordered a long time in advance; butter, for instance, coming in kegs from Australia. The climate was so damp that shoes went mouldy in their racks, and without a daily inspection would grow fungus. When Nesta visited the nearest dentist — an American — she had to be carried in a litter by coolies for miles over mountain paths.

"They lived in Chungking for four years until the 1914 war broke out and Kenneth returned home to join up. This meant a nightmare journey across Siberia to St Petersburg to find a ship bound for England. The experience left Nesta very shaken and nervous. Kenneth trained for the artillery at Weedon and was sent to France but, much to his disappointment, was put in charge of Chinese road-builders because he could speak their language. Nesta underwent an operation from which she did not recover, and I lost one of my best friends. Ella outlived her daughters by many years, and died at 87."

Edward Arthur, Teddy's sixth son, took up medicine, studied in Edinburgh and practised in Leicester where he was greatly loved as a doctor and was much in demand for concerts, as he had a fine singing voice and played the violin with his younger brother Evan. He married Elizabeth Strachan whom he met while studying, but died early when his heart could not withstand an illness contracted in the course of his work. Doris recalls: ''His funeral was one to be remembered. He was buried beside his parents, and so many mourners attended that the cortege stretched for two miles from Desborough station to Rothwell.'' The children were Philip, Madge and Ruth. Philip studied medicine and law, and became assistant to Ingleby Oddie, the Central London coroner who regularly conducted inquests attracting wide public attention including the R101 airship disaster and many famous cases in the history of crime.

Teddy and Elizabeth must have given up hope of a daughter, but their seventh new arrival changed the sequence. She was Ada, in later years a companion for her father as he drove round on business. She married Harry Butlin, son of J. T. Butlin the Rothwell shoe manufacturer and captain in the Volunteers. During her first pregnancy they were staying at Teddy's farm at Thorpe Underwood where the family spent spring and summer. In the midst of a snowstorm unseasonably on St George's Day (April 23), Ada felt the onset of labour pains, and Harry had to struggle through drifts to Rothwell to get Dr More. By the time the doctor arrived baby Norman had been safely born. In later years he and his brother Paul ran the Rothwell factory. Edward became a schoolmaster, and the fourth son Alfred was connected with the True Form company.

Number eight was Teddy's second daughter Martha (Pat). Her young life was upset by a romantic interlude. She played the mandoline and harp, and fell in love with a musician she met at a concert. She ran away with him, but two of her brothers followed the pair and brought Pat home. No more was heard of the affair. Allyn Longland, whom she married later, was also a harpist and accompanied Pat when she sang at concerts. She used her sweet soprano voice to further many good causes, raising £1,000 during the First World War for national charities — possibly approaching a quarter of a million today. Pat's son Fred was the strong man of the family. He could bend a poker, tear directories in halves, and support someone standing on his upturned calf.

Left a widow, Pat was cared for in advancing years by her daughter Cissie, also a widow, who in her old age had to have both legs removed. She kept cheerful with the help of two daughters who bought an estate car so that they could take her about in her wheelchair.

It was back to sons with Luther, Teddy's ninth, whom Doris describes as a character. He started his working life as a butcher, but contracted anthrax and almost died. Recovering, he became a Wesleyan missionary and went to Barbados, rearing his family there. Needing a new chapel he came to Kettering and Rothwell and in less than a year raised enough money to build it, sending back photographs when the chapel was completed. He joined up at the start of the 1914 war, gained rapid promotion and was posted to India as a colonel. After the war he stayed on as a tea planter, and his four children lived mainly abroad.

Polly and Fan, numbers ten and eleven, trained as nurses at St Bartholomew's. Polly married the secretary of the hospital, and Fan married Dr Kirkland Chapel who became assistant to Dr Allison at Kettering, looking after Rothwell patients at the newly-built house and surgery in Tresham Street. Later they moved to Leicester.

The tally ends on a humorous note, thanks to Evan the twelfth and last of Teddy and Elizabeth's quiverful. He became a solicitor, and as official receiver for Leicester was in charge of the Sir Arthur Wheeler case, a sensational failure of 1931. Owing to pressure of work Evan forgot to obtain the licence for his wedding to a Leicester bride, and guests who arrived at the church waited in vain. They were conducted instead to the reception, where explanations and apologies were forthcoming, and one gathers that a good time was had by all. The nuptials took place quietly next day. Evan and his wife Ethel reared five children — Morgan, a redoubtable member of Leicester Tigers, two who became schoolmasters, and two daughters of whom Joyce became a painter of miniatures.

Fred Moore caps the forgotten-licence story. His great-grandfather was working for Teddy Barlow when they built St Andrew's Church, and Teddy gave him the job of hanging the bell. Hoisting and mounting it presented problems, and to plan the operation James Moore locked himself in the one place where he could concentrate undisturbed — the lavatory at his home in School Lane. The rest of the family had to wait with their problems unsolved for an hour and a half.

THE WRIGHTS

The story of the Wrights, one of the leading shoemaking and sporting families, has been re-created by Ted Wright who returned to Kettering after a career as a Whitehall scientific civil servant. He is the younger son of Horace (Hob) Wright who for many years ran the George Wright business in Tresham Street.

Founder of the family was John David Wright, a mid-Victorian handsewn shoemaker and an active member of Rockingham Road Wesleyan Church, which he brought up his children to support generously. John's wife Martha (née Turner) gave him five sons and two daughters, of whom three sons were to play distinguished parts in the Kettering shoe industry at the peak of its success. Frank, George and Henry were sent to learn shoemaking by machinery, and all founded firms. The other children were Horace who farmed at Wymington, Myra, Walter and Mary. Mary married Jim Christie whose market gardens off Britannia Road have since been built over.

George was the first of John's sons to venture into business. He established George Wright (Kettering) Ltd in 1891 with E. C. Gravestock, who was also a pillar of the Wesleyan church. They started in School Lane, then built the Tresham Street factory. George bought out Gravestock, who founded E. C. Gravestock Ltd of Avenue Works, St Peters Avenue.

Maud Mitchell, whose family was connected with Kettering Brick & Tile Co., became Mrs George Wright, and there were 14 children of whom 12 survived. The second son, Arthur James (AJ to the family, who often shortened names to initials) chose an academic career, started the family tradition of taking a Cambridge degree, and was teaching at Wellingborough School when the 1914-18 war broke out. He became a brigade-major in the Northamptonshire Regiment and won the MC and DSO at Gallipoli.

Hob, Steve and Albert went into the business with their father and all joined up, eventually leaving George to carry on alone. Hob was first a despatch rider, taking his own motorcycle to France, then was seconded to the artillery as a battery supplies officer. Steve served in the county regiment and then as a Royal Flying Corps lieutenant in the Middle East campaign. Albert was a cadet at Sandhurst when the war ended.

After the armistice, AJ, who remained single, became senior master at Wellingborough School and housemaster at Fryers. Hob, Steve and Albert returned to George Wright's and Hob took over as managing director when his father moved to Bournemouth in the 1920s. He married Margery Barlow, daughter of Fred Barlow the Rothwell and Kettering builder. Norah Wright, a cousin, became Steve's wife, and Albert married Mollie Allingham. George's other children were Maud (m. Ernest Foster of Smith & Foster), George (GR, the eldest son, m. Hilda Hawthorne), Ernest (m. Mary Dyke), Olive, Constance (m. Ted Seddon), Violet (m. Sid Seddon), Dick (m. Dolly Mabelson) and Sidney.

With their father, GR and Ernest became directors of another footwear firm, W. Nichols & Son Ltd, which they acquired in 1913. The owners were a Raunds family, and the business, dating from the Napoleonic wars, was said to be the oldest on the War Office list of contractors. The Wrights moved it to larger premises in Havelock Street where it was known as "the army shop" because it specialised in Service boots. After war broke out in 1914 the factory worked night and day for many months, helping to meet the demand for boots for the new armies.

The children of GR and Hilda were George Henson (m. Diana Stokes, daughter of Boots' manager Walter Stokes) and Eve. Ernest and Mary's daughter Mollie married Eddie Knapper and lives in Bath. Ted and Constance Seddon's son John served in the last war with the Navy, retiring as lieutenant-commander in 1954 when he moved into printing. Constance, in her 90s, lives near him at Marton, Gainsborough. Sid and Violet Seddon had two children, Paul and Louisa (m. Angus McKinnon). Paul took a degree at Cambridge, then was commissioned in the Royal Engineers. After demobilisation he married Monica Mobbs, and with their two sons developed Seddon Packaging & Print, originally Seddons & Arlidge, carton-makers. Paul served for many years as chairman of Kettering Health Authority, is chairman of Kettering magistrates, and High Sheriff of Northamptonshire.

Olive remained unmarried after a tragic blow during the 1914-18 war. She received two telegrams, the first telling her that fiance Dicky Bird was safe, and the second reporting his death in action. She accompanied her father in his retirement to Bournemouth, and lived to 93.

Dick was the first of the Wright county cricketers, showing his mettle against Notts at Nortampton in 1925 by scoring 103 off a deadly attack including Larwood, the demon fast bowler who figured in the bodyline controversy during the Australia Tests. He was equally gifted at football, captaining Kettering Town in 1924 when the Poppies met Gillingham in two gripping FA Cup matches. More than 9,000 packed the Rockingham Road ground for the first game which ended 1-1 after the referee had sent off the Poppies' star forward Cotton. A crowd gathered round the dressing room for words with the referee, but Cotton apologised for over-enthusiasm, and the ref got away unobtrusively. Dick was the star of the replay, scoring both Kettering goals, but Gillingham netted six. In 1926 he went to Canada, worked in the Mobbs & Lewis forestry enterprises, came back in the second world war as a Canadian Air Force sergeant stationed in Hampshire, and after demob played for Hampshire 2nd XI in the intervals of establishing a chain of fish and chip shops along the South Coast. Sidney stayed single, worked in the Canadian forests with Dick, and eventually joined his father in Bournemouth.

Henry Wright started in business in 1892 as H. Wright & Sons, home and export manufacturers, assisted by sons Dennis, Ernest (EV) and Harold. EV joined the Royal Fusiliers in September 1914 and saw much service on the Western Front. He transferred to the Motor Machine Gun Corps and so to tanks, winning the MC at Cambrai in 1917. This was the first mass assault by tanks and, as there were no radios then, the officers walked into the attack and directed the tanks to their objectives under rifle and machine-gun fire. He married Marie, daughter of Mr and Mrs Charles Clarke, whose son Louis was killed in the war. There were two children. John took a Cambridge degree in engineering and was awarded a travelling fellowship by Christs College to study in the USA. He did national service as an engineer officer in the Navy and worked at Satra for 25 years. He remained single and looks after his mother who, at the time of writing, is 95. Judith (m. John Walker) lives in Norfolk.

Henry's daughters were Norah who married Steve, and Edith who became Mrs Alexander. Steve and Norah had three children — Mary, a staff nurse at Leicester Royal Infirmary, David who served as a regular chief petty officer in the Fleet Air Arm and afterwards joined the British Aircraft Corporation, and Pamela who was on the domestic staff at Kettering General Hospital.

Frank and Henry established F. Wright and Co. (Kettering) in 1895. They split up in 1905 for Frank, who married Eva West, to carry on the business with sons Frank (FA) and Bertie. Both served in the 1914 war. FA, a major in the Northamptonshire Regiment, was one of the handful of officers who came through the Gallipoli campaign, and Bertie gained the MC as a lieutenant in the 7th Northants. FA married Ruth Dunn, and died in 1923 from the effects of mustard gas poisoning. Bertie's wife was Doris Perkins. The other members of the family were Winnie (m. Harold 'Aribo' Hales), May (m. Frank Everard), Ethel ('Pete', m. Stewart Mackay), Nicholas Edward (m. Marjorie Neale), Philip (PA, m. Jessie Pretty), Stella (m. 1 Rex Gent, killed serving with the RAF during the war, 2 Bill Parker), and Nona the ninth child (m. Prof. Joseph Doupe of Manitoba). Winnie at 99 lives near her grandson in the West Country, and Ethel still living in Kettering is 92.

Those were the days of large families, and Mrs Graham Campbell (née Jane Mackay), one of Frank's granddaughters, recalls an occasion when the number of relatives was totted up. There were around 250, most of whom were still living in the district. In 1921 the family placed a tablet in Rockingham Road Church with the inscription:

> In remembrance of John David Wright 1839-1909 and of Martha his wife 1843-1919 who for many years were devoted members of this Church and Congregation, this tablet was placed here by their family as a token of gratitude for the safe return of their sons (grandsons of the above) from the Great War 1914-1919, fifteen of whom served in

His Majesty's Forces, one only, Second Lieutenant J. G. Christy, falling in action at Magny la Fosse, October 3rd, 1918.

The Wrights' skill at games was proverbial. Besides Dick, those who played cricket for Northants in the 1920s were Albert, AJ, Steve, Nick, Bertie and PA. PA captained Wellingborough

FRIDAY, SEPTEMBER 19, 1919   8

A UNIQUE KETTERING FAMILY.

From Left to Right:—Back Row: G. R. Wright, F. A. Wright, junr., A. J. Wright, D.S.O., M.C., E. V. Wright, M.C., N. E. Wright.
Middle Row: S. Wright, T. H. Wright, Geo. Wright, E. Wright, F. A. Wright, B. Wright, M.C., A. Wright.
Front Row: R. L. Wright, P. A. Wright.
In another part of this issue we give details of an interesting cricket match played last Saturday on the Kettering cricket ground, between fourteen members of the Wright family, of Kettering, and fourteen members of the Kettering Cricket Club, in aid of the Kettering and District General Hospital. The Wrights won. It may be recalled that six years ago a similar match was arranged, in which eleven of those who took part in Saturday's match figured in the Wright team which met the Town Club for the same charitable purpose. On that occasion the Wrights finished on the wrong side. In the interim, no fewer than eight of the Wright family served through the great campaign, several, it will be noted, with distinction. The sporting proclivities of Messrs. George Wright and Frank Wright, and their generous work for charity, are well known, and, as we announced last week, they have this season figured very prominently in international bowls. In fact, the Wrights are as Right as Right can be—business men, sportsmen, soldiers, and gentlemen.

A tattered newspaper cutting records the Wright family's cricket win over Kettering Town in the 1919 challenge match.   (Fred Moore)

School in 1921, and played for Public Schools versus the Army at Lord's. In three years at Cambridge he took 157 wickets, and was also a soccer blue. J. D. Coldham in his *Northamptonshire Cricket* says PA's bowling looked straightforward, but in fact was most difficult, swerving from leg at the last moment and coming up devilishly from a responsive pitch.

The Wrights played Kettering Town twice at cricket. The first game, before 1914, saw them defeated. Most of the eleven family players served in the war, and in 1919 to mark their safe return issued a challenge for a repeat game to aid the hospital. Fourteen Wrights wanted to take part, so two XIV sides faced one another and the Wrights won by 107 runs to 70. The Kettering CC centenary book notes that town cricket in the 1920s was dominated by the Wrights who could field a complete XI including PA who was a University and County all-rounder of the highest class. In other sports AJ was a Cambridge half-blue at golf and tennis, Hob and Jack (Horace's son) played hockey for the town, and Maud's daughter Barbara, sister of Muriel and Billy, played tennis for the County.

The family sporting talent came from George and Frank, who as young men took part in many contests, even racing one another up Rockingham Hill on ordinary (penny-farthing) bicycles for a 5s bet. George played for Kettering Town FC in its early days besides helping with administration. Running, boxing and billiards attracted him, and he served as chairman of the Hospital Sports Committee which each year staged an attractive one-day fixture on Northampton Road recreation ground, relied on to raise a major share of the hospital costs.

George and Frank were so keen on billiards that they built billiard rooms on to their houses. George's first was at Ivy House, London Road, and when he moved to Belle Vue off Broadway he retained the right to use Ivy House billiard room until his new one was ready. Frank used to engage top-line players Lindrum and Davis to play him in his billiard room at Petherton House, Rockingham Road. He was a member of the Victoria Sporting Club in London and won its billiards championship.

Both the brothers were international bowls players. Locally George played for the Lodge, helped to set up the factory bowls league, and provided its silver trophy, now in the museum. He won the county and national bowls championships, and in

1925-26 captained the first English bowls Test team to play Australia and New Zealand. As president of the English Bowls Association he visited Australia, New Zealand, South Africa, Canada and the United States.

Anecdotes about members of the family give a clue to their characters. Hob and Margery never lost their figures, and on each major anniversary of their wedding used to don their carefully preserved morning suit and bridal gown and invite family and friends to a champagne luncheon. The custom carried on until the 65th anniversary, when their outfits still fitted. They were persuaded to lend the clothes for the 1975 Town and Country exhibition in Kettering Art Gallery, and I remember the pleasure with which they stood hand in hand looking at "themselves when young" — display figures wearing the wedding finery and posed against a photo background of many family celebrations down the years.

During the 1930s depression, George Wright employees agreed with Hob that they would take a voluntary cut in wages from 56s to 54s a week. The directors — himself, Steve and Albert — took cuts in proportion, and published on the works notice board their take-home pay. During the last war Hob's national service in addition to his work as managing director of the firm was running the Auxiliary Fire Service station at the bottom of London Road hill, which sent back-up pumps to the Coventry blitz.

At one hospital fete in the 1930s the George Wright float was "Take a peek at Lady Godiva." Would-be peeping Toms paid their money and were escorted by Hob and Albert between obscuring panels to view Steve, appropriately undressed with flowing tresses, holding a statuesque pose on horseback.

Whenever Frank went to London on business, he was immaculately turned out, and always carried the regulation rolled umbrella. One day PA had to go instead and, as the weather was threatening, he grabbed his father's umbrella. It was raining in London, and emerging from St Pancras he unfurled the umbrella, only to see it crumble to bare ribs, the fabric falling all over him. Frank always used taxis and never opened his brolly, which through many years had been a feast for moths.

Ted remembers the sad occasion in 1951 when Hob, then president of the Kettering Shoe Manufacturers Association, told his colleagues and rivals that after an analysis of George Wright's financial position and the increasing threat from cheap moulded footwear the company had decided to go into voluntary liquidation rather than attempt to raise capital to re-equip and carry on. He exhorted his fellow manufacturers to look at their prospects with a similarly critical eye.

With Steve, Albert and the staff who included Walter Bell, Hob set about liquidation. Munn & Feltons bought the factory, and everyone on the payroll was either found a job elsewhere or given a retirement annuity — something Ted is proud to recall. While this was proceeding, Hob and Margery built their retirement house, 30 Pipers Hill Road, in the kitchen garden of their old home, 119 London Road. Ted, who was born in the London Road house, succeeded his parents in Pipers Hill Road, and feels he has completed full circle by "returning to his natal cabbage patch." He carried on the tradition by taking a Cambridge degree, and with his elder brother Jimmy was one of the Barlow family connections recorded by Doris Butlin as undergoing disastrous war experiences but miraculously surviving.

Ted was a captain in the County regiment, and Jimmy a captain with a Royal Engineers field survey unit in advance of the front line. Both were hospitalised. Ted, when seconded to the Somerset Light Infantry and taking part in the final push into Germany was hit by shrapnel intended for supporting tanks, which he found afterwards were commanded by Captain Nick Wide, MC, also from Kettering. Jimmy was for many months in Naples military hospital.

Later in life Jimmy became chairman and managing director of a brickworks at Telford, automated under his guidance. Ted, remembering grandma Maud Mitchell and the Kettering brickworks, has changed the old saying about clogs to "bricks to bricks in three generations."

The more recent history of Frank Wright Shoes is filled in by Neil Wright, son of Nicholas (NE) and Frank's grandson. Neil says he is the one remaining "shoemaker" of the family, still in the business of marketing footwear as sales director of Griggs of Wollaston, now owners of the former Gravestock factory in Kettering, established by George Wright's partner of a century ago.

Frank, who died in 1958, bought the quality sports footwear firm of Mobbs Bros. (Embekay), Durban Road, and J. W. Black of South Wigston who made ladies' shoes. From the 1960s other companies purchased were Pit-a-Pat, Wellingborough, makers of children's sandal shoes, Wilson & Watson, Towell & Co., and Dalkeith Shoes, the last three forming the Shire Shoes Group. Acquired about the same time was the Coles Group of Burton Latimer, and two Leicester firms taken over were Gidley Wright and Diana Shoes. Neil joined Frank Wright in 1959 when it was being run by John Mackay, another of Frank's grandsons whose wife Pamela was a granddaughter of William Timpson.

At this time Frank Wright Shoes was able to supply whatever styles were in demand, from heavy crepe-soled Teddy Boy shoes to Italian pointed-toe styles known as "winkle-pickers", and from platform shoes for men to cowboy boots. The fashion business was very successful, exports going to many parts of the world. Testimony to their wide appeal came from the firm's Norwegian agent who supplied a retailer north of the Arctic Circle. One day a stranger called wearing a pair of Frank Wright fashion shoes, and the retailer found he was a tourist who had bought them in Australia.

Embekay at first was run by Neil's father, NE, and his uncle PA, known as Nick and Bill. Their topical brand names included the Billy Wright soccer boot and the Peter May cricket boot. One to test the knowledge of current sports fans was the pre-1939 Charlie Buchan soccer boot. During the last war the firm made special military footwear. Outsize boots were required for the Sudanese Camel Corps who had very large feet due to walking shoeless on sand, and size 17 H fitting were not uncommon.

Hob Wright — TH to the family — wore a stern expression when in his office or walking round the factory which, in the Kettering tradition of expressive labels, earned him the nickname of "The Laughing Cavalier". But he had an engaging off-duty smile, shown in 1951 when he was president of the Kettering Boot Manufacturers' Association.
(Evening Telegraph)

Aircrew boots were shearling lined for warmth, and had a pocket holding a very sharp penknife. If the wearer was shot down he could cut the boot to ankle height so that it was easier to walk in and less noticeable. Just two examples of specialist skills in the Kettering shoe trade.

Like many other manufacturers the Frank Wright group eventually fell prey to the influx of cheap fashion shoes from the Far East, closing down in the 1980s. But the name continues. Alan Everard, a former director of the Shire Group and the last managing director of Frank Wright Shoes acquired the title and part of the company, now based at Burton Latimer as Frank Wright (Footwear) Ltd. Alan is nephew of Frank Everard, Frank Wright's son-in-law, so the family link carries on.